T0208880

Don't Kill the Messenger 69...
the chronicles of Jo

JIMMY CHAN

authorHOUSE®

AuthorHouse™
1663 Liberty Drive
Bloomington, IN 47403
www.authorhouse.com
Phone: 1 (800) 839-8640

Published by AuthorHouse 04/24/2015

ISBN: 978-1-5049-0104-8 (sc)
ISBN: 978-1-5049-0105-5 (e)

Library of Congress Control Number: 2015903990

Print information available on the last page.

Any people depicted in stock imagery provided by Thinkstock are models, and such images are being used for illustrative purposes only. Certain stock imagery © Thinkstock.

This book is printed on acid-free paper.

Because of the dynamic nature of the Internet, any web addresses or links contained in this book may have changed since publication and may no longer be valid. The views expressed in this work are solely those of the author and do not necessarily reflect the views of the publisher, and the publisher hereby disclaims any responsibility for them.

Contents

My Morning and Evening Prayer

In the spirit of bringing in a New Year

I wish you all peace, love, prosperity and harmony with self and your fellow man. May wisdom pro and precede knowledge. May you hear the voices of the ancestors who whisper in the wind guiding you to your higher self. May Love conquer all shapes and forms of hate. May the mind of a child not be tainted by those who have not found or have chosen to let go of the essence of purity and the connection to God. May God have mercy on mans soul for his role in the polluting and destruction of this planet we call home and may she shine a light so brightly that all who have been asleep will finally awaken and step forward to help in the chanting away of all negative and evil forces that resides in mans heart.

Mandarin and Cantonese Chinese
Gong Hay Fat Choy (Gung Xi Fat Cai)
(Best wishes and Congratulations. Have a prosperous and good year)

Sanskrit

नववर्षाभिनन्दनम्

(Happy New Year)

Swahili
Furaha ya mwaka mpya
(Happy New Year)
Maisha marefu! Afya! Vifijo!
(Cheers/Good Health)

Welcome into the Year of The Sheep!
These writings are from the chronicles of my spirit self.
I am
Fo Flight69

Words About the Author

"Chan is my friend and spiritual gentle giant! He has given us the tools to govern and express our minds, bodies and soul..."

Rebecca Pope
Athlete and T.V. Technical Director

"You are a unique and gentle spirit. A remarkable being that I feel blessed to have met! Your soul is beautiful and writing style truly incredible! You are an inspiration!"

Missy Reid
Athlete/Writer

"Jimmy Chan represents the true definition of what a friend should be. Always listening, always asking, always caring and always sharing. He has inspired me through his actions to believe harder, try harder and love harder. We have traveled, shared, worked, taught, created and performed together all over the world! I am blessed to have him in my life not only as a friend but also as a brother. Here's to our next adventure together!"

Josh Misegades
Actor/Stage Crew Manager for Cirque Du Soleil

"Jimmy Chan is my friend and guru both physically and spiritually. It has been a Great Journey together"

Nancy Foxx
Athlete/Artist/Mother/Survivor

"Thank you for being the crazy man that you are! Giving, funny and strangely balanced!"

Elaine Travlos
Athlete/Photographer/Caterer

"Once in a while a person comes along in your life and touches you so deeply and on different levels. Jimmychan is that person. Chan is one of the most rare and fascinating persons I've ever known. He is wise beyond his years and makes you believe his soul has been around the block more than a few times. Chan is energetic, compassionate and has an infectious love for life. He is a true artist and visionary."

Christine Pardy
Singer/Actor/Mom

"When Jimmy comes to our home, with him, he brings sunshine, enthusiasm, love and a wonderful spirit! We love his big heart that embraces life and genuine love for people."

Jeff Foxx
Broker/Athlete/Father

"As I sit here listening to Gnarls Barkley's 'Crazy', I think about how we, you and I are possibly viewed by our white and black folks. But if crazy allows me, allows you, to leave an Artistic Imprint of our souls on the world then it's worth the crazy ride! You remind me of Ce-Lo because you have that creative, beautiful outside the box thinking! Thank you for Being Crazy Beautiful, I love You! Thank you for kicking my ass and making me write my book along with my family!"

Khrysy Renfro-Stella
Athlete/Artist/Mom

"As Buddha says, 'we are formed and molded by our thoughts. Those whose minds are shaped by selfless thoughts give joy when they speak or act. Joy follows them like a shadow that never leaves them.' This best describes Jimmy Chan. He has an enthusiasm for life that is limitless and a spirit that leaves a trail of joy wherever he travels. His love for all people shines like a ray of sunshine through his encouraging words of selfless attitude. His discipline speaks of all hard work he has done in becoming the best person he can be-physically, mentally and spiritually.
Thank you for sharing your amazing spirit with us".
Your Sherwood Family

Acknowledgement

First and foremost, I'd like to thank God, my Higher Self for allowing this fire to reside within me! There are so many ways of articulating through motion and language. I thank God for giving me yet another way of expressing my feelings, thoughts and emotions through this organic energy known as my spirit! I thank my brother Herman for continuing this rocky road of a journey known as life while staying true as blood and spirit brothers. Somewhere in our time things shall define themselves truly as God's truth. I hope to be standing by your side when the gate opens. Though she doesn't know, C Lea Pea, the Muse has affected me such a way, I can't seem to be able to put the pen down. But then why stop this that is right? I dream of you always and with those dreams so continues the streams! More on you in a moment! ☺ Thank you Phil Resnick for being one of the coolest persons on the planet to ever work for or with. You just surprise me every time and I still don't know how to repay you for such kind gestures. As always, I am there for you whenever you need me come rain, sleet or shine! Mad love and respect to you and your family! Thank you Aaron and Sheila Cohen for believing in me while others would become cold and turn their backs. Thanks for sharing your wisdom and joy for life without casting judgment upon me. Thanks for coming out to my show at the Little Black Pearl and celebrating with me the release of my first book Streams of Consciousness 69Times. What a night! Much love and respect! Let's keep training!

I'd like to thank my mom for stepping forward and being herself while allowing me to be me while we become reacquainted and live within our new found harmony. Pause that thought! I'll get back to you! LOL

Special thanks to U.S.A. Shaolin Temple for the Chi! Shifu, you are the Buddha that helped me search for and find mine. I hope somewhere within these centuries of our training, I make you proud! Thank you for allowing me to fulfill yet another dream, Teaching at the temple! I feel like the Prodigal Son from the movie "Master Killer" who has been sent out on a mission

Wu Shifu, thank you for your continued education in the beautiful art of Tai Ji Quan! It's been 20 years now! You have always been an inspiration to me and I hope to continue training within your lineage. Please tell my aunties and uncles in Las Vegas that I said hello and look forward to training and demonstrating your teachings by their side. I look forward to your return to Chicago so we can start spring training! As you would always say, "No Lazy!"

Special thanks to Rising Phoenix, Chicago, Il. (Catherine Shifu and Pat Shifu)for allowing me a place to train and teach Tai Ji.You both have been so supportive throughout my endeavors as students, teachers and most importantly as friends! Thank you for sharing the chi and just being two of the coolest phoenix's I could want to hang and train with!

Buddha bless you!

Crazy thank you goes out to Michele Timkang and Richards Career Academy for allowing me to step into the halls and share this crazy brand of teaching TaiJi and Poetry! What an incredible impact we've made over these past 3 years with some students who have demonstrated levels of "Pure Genius"! I'm working on getting the Exodus Program started up and running as soon as possible.

Thank you Josh Misegades for believing in my work! What an incredible journey we've shared so far! Since back in 98' when we first met overseas that has taken us to and from Paris, Italia, New York, Chicago, Iowa, Michigan, California and Las Vegas...where shall we meet up next? Thanks for introducing me to Cirque du Soliel's Ka and Iris group. It was an awesome experience being able to come and share my work and just be in the presence of such incredibly talented people! Whenever they want me again, just say the word and I'm there! One crazy mad respect to you for coming to Chicago at the last minute and performing with me at the Little Black Pearl!
Yet another story to be told!!! I love you my brother! I will see you real soon!!!

Thank you Andy O'Beirne! Thank you for your continued support and friendship throughout these 15 years and allowing me a place to lay my head every time I find my way there on the East Coast! You are truly a friend that I am blessed to have in my life.

Thank you Mom, for all of the conversations on the phone loaded with encouragement wisdom and love! I could write an entire book just on our conversations, alone! Know that I love you with all of my heart and look forward to spending more quality time with you face to face with all of us, your kids basking in your beauty! Soon Herman and I shall be as one again.

Herman Kelly, You my Brother are so full of love that I need in my life and look forward to the day when we can be back in our circle and laughing ourselves to tears! I Love you Big Brother like no one could ever comprehend! May we continue this journey living in love!

Last and absolutely not the least, I would like to thank Chrissy Lea! Wow, you have stood by me when all else would run and you just gave me Pure Love! You have literally been an angelic figure chasing all of my demons away just because of a simple word. Love! How do I adore you? None could ever measure. Thank you for taking me on this journey known as forever loving you! Next stop, Australia! You are my friend, lover, partner, companion, camera crew, guru and healer all rolled up into one big beautiful you! From the depths of my heart, always know that I love you truly and deeply!

Foreword

Welcome to the Dragons Den!

Life offers many lessons for one to learn, observe, and adhere to. The pathway one takes evolves a constant connection to its internal and external functions. And, the universe patiently waits for the chosen to illuminate within the 'present' dark ages of the unconscious mind with programmed technological behaviors design to disconnect our social responsibilities. These lessons of life within the pages of Don't Kill The Messenger…the chronicles of Fo offers such insight and guidance. The focal point for the reader is to 'possibly' find oneself within the pages and intrinsically grow while building their environment, physically and spiritually.

Next, there is a diversity pertaining to Jimmy Chan aka Fo Flight69's methodology of expression. If you only can READ with the *eye* of overstanding, concern, ambitions, enthusiasm, endurance, humbleness, discipline, courage, love, truth, peace, freedom, and justice (13). The aspects of diversity will reverberate with all (7) of one's chakras while offering a clear pathway toward enlightenment. As the sun, moon, and stars align themselves to bring forth this message. I challenge each reader to set aside the many aspects of the matrix and indulge yourself within the words of the author, in hopes, of reaching your inner-most needs, wants, and aspirations.

Finally, may the four elements of the universe continually offer insight for the reader while the ancient lessons are learned. **Fire** is purifying. It offers a means to reflect upon the needs of the self (South), **Water** is used for healing and cleansing (West), **Air** directly unites the essence and the breath of existence (East), and **Earth** gives stability (North). These are the elements that govern all of us.

Blessings,

Noble Dr. Ahmose Mustapha Anu Hughes-Bey

Amitabha

Chicago June 2007

the Buddha is the mind
so many fail in understanding it's teachings because
they often attempt to find
answers to questions that aren't in line with their center

you must practice spring, summer, fall and winter
this member of the center is the actual mastermind
connecting the Dan Tien at your belly to
the dome that sits atop your spine
the human equivalent to a computer chip
if not stacked properly
you could slip a disk or
at the very least, constantly trip over your own two feet
into the third eye you must be willing to peak
material possessions should not be what you seek
to find balance
you should practice sitting in silence and
just hear you breathe
to master the mind you must be willing to roll up your sleeves
how long will this battle ensue?
which side of you shall you turn to?
within every man there lies a struggle he battles through
once you've reached that moment of enlightenment
may you hear
you
deep inside

Amitabha Amitabha Amitabha

My Chant

Don't try to make I stop
Don't even try to block
I say no o o o o o!

say I won't take a stop
till I reach the top
I say no o o o o o o o!

here I come with a plan
got no pistol in my hand

I say
no o o o o o o o o o!

when you hear me sing this song
won't you join in and sing along
say o o o o o o o o o o o o o o o!
I've become a wiser a man
since I came to understand
the rivers how they deeply flow!

sip from the precious pure water
so you can grow

I man gonna take it easy
I man gonna take it slow
say o o o o o o o o o!

I say don't you know
man you reaping what you sow
don't you know!
don't try to make 3rd eye stop
I'm about to reach the top
here we go o o o o o o o o o o o!

Incense

Chicago May 2012

Light incense 1, 2 and 3
For the mind, body and spirit
Each breathes
Blessings be given to humanity
Through these resins burns hope radiating throughout 69 galaxies x 3 to infinity
I humbly light 3
One for Shifu
Another for Shaolin Temple
The 3rd, well for me
While walking these crazy ass Chicago and New York streets
I was training in the temple and Kha West said,
"Hey Fo, I got this beat and I want you to spit on it for me"
incense 1, 2 and 3
so many lessons are taught but who's learning?
In the blink of an eye somebody's confirming
a corpse is found because of a savage yearning
1, 2 and 3 incense are burning
while bombs are built and delivering
destroying, employing destruction
Babylon enjoying his reconstruction
Man it looks like an abduction
Invasion of the body snatchers is so much more than a production
I light 1, 2 and 3 incense trusting
Keeping me from lusting
Too much cussing
Light 108 up in smoke

Every piece of poetry I ever wrote then spoke
Meditate to the slow float
Just before it bolts and gets caught into the wind tunnel
To be funneled into the nose cavity
A meditation from me equals we
Third eye being internally centered
Making it truly the one that can see
I can hear the sparks as the resins and wood turn to debris
I can smell the pungy aroma of sandalwood emitting
It's getting kind of tricky

Cause I like to burn while I'm spitting

Nag Champa just happens to be the aroma that you're sniffing

We're all getting older so count your blessings cause

Soon will come the day when we become those boulders of cosmic dust

In the wind to begin and become an even finer blend

Light incense 1, 2 and 3 for the mind, body and soul

Like the smoke flowing in the air to be free

I light incense 1, 2 and 3 and until they burn out

I continue to flow like the smoke while training in some Tai Chi

Light incense 1, 2 and 3

I light one for God, One for the universe and to all living within this celestial tree

Light incense 1, 2, and 3

One for the little girl who was just killed

Her blood was spilled and these wounds will never heal

For the monks who burned themselves alive

On them China city streets

So many have lost their lives and have become deceased

I light these incense 1, 2 and 3

Sitting in silence

Meditating on peace, love and non-violence

Incense 1, 2 and 3

Lit for making in-sense

To all that I've harmed or have disrupted their harmony and rhythm

Within this prism of smolder resins

A promise to self

is to always carry self like a sweet aroma within another presence

I light these incense 1, 2 and 3 humbly

Sharing this crazy ass energy!

1, 2 and 3

for the Black Butterflies camouflaged in them big oak trees

for the victims of any tsunami

I light incense 1, 2 and 3

Peace, Love and Wisdom

Merry Christmas

Chicago December 24, 2012

Maybe you didn't get all that you wanted for Christmas
A gift list to make the average person broke as shit!
Skip giving actual love cause it just don't kiss God enough
So that's dismissed
From the west to the Brits
Help feed the homeless with some gravy and grits
If you got them
Rib tips unless they're vegan
then feed them with the Sanskrit's
Back it up with some of the Old Testament with asparagus tips, carrots and
Lettuce sip the water that Jesus changed into wine to Holy trip Bat Man
How is it possible that homelessness and poverty still exists?
Babylon has a tight grip and don't want to share Mama Earth's gifts
This has become my home
Will someone give or loan me a few dollars?
So I can go to a shelter cause I'm frozen to the bone
My family has disowned me so there is no one to phone
Maybe FEMA has been shown that
I'm right here!
In Need
Merry Christmas…

Peace Love Wisdom

The Art of War

New York 2011

Gaze into the Sun Tzu
Like The Guns of Navarone
The Art of War Is Upon you
The Master Killer's Gordon Liu shall teach you real gung fu!
The Rasta wheeling them machete in them Blue Mountains
Smoking flaming refer!
Forged in fire like the Bushido Blade of Sunny Chiba
Night creepers dressed as Ninjas to put you in a permanent sleepers hold!
Bold tactics taught by aged old sages
Who demonstrate "Lazy Monk Tucks His Robe"
The best revenge is that dish served cold!
Behold
The Art of War

Peace Be Still

New York May 2011

It's time to swallow the pill
The blue or the red was the choice and now its time to fulfill
The prophecy that would bury you in a landfill
Bury you alive like in "Kill Bill"
Beatrice chose the path of some skills
Bruised knuckles of the one inch punch that would shatter your spin
While the intestines would fill with bile
who come to feel?
While we take you on a lyrical flow
Byrds of a Feather blowing on that saxophone so
USA Shaolin Temple Demo Team
Coming in like thieves in the night
Ninja flows that creep into your eardrum like that double edged knife
Piercing right into your cerebellum
Tell 'em, peace be still little grass hopper
This could be an instant heart stopper
Show popper!
To sit still in meditation you must be in a proper state of mind
Fo Flight's about to help you find your inner groove
While we keep this real smooth
Byrds of a Feather flocking together
Looking up into the full moon
Hey Siete, Can you hear 'em croon?
Peace be still
While we feel this instant classic of a groove!
Shaolin Temple!

Every breath breathed comes out like a monsoon
This is where Gung Fu and Tai Chi flex the best
I get to flow to some of this smooth shit!
While I summon this lyrical fest of
Cranes Fist Swallowing the Monkey's Fruit while He Takes a Piss!
Man, kiss my ass!

while I teach this lyrical ballet class of Mad Max's road rage bash
Toke on some of that hash that creates this thunder in my dome
Flown in on Mt. Olympus
You think this shit ain't real?

Haters step forward so I can lyrically pimp slap you in the grill
Coming straight from Shaolin Snake Spits its Tongue skills
Lyrically clocking your ass
Searching for that weak spot then I'm gonna drill
Like BP, I'm going so deep into the core
You're gonna spill every drop of your ill will
Dim Mak is the touch of death that can leave you paralyzed, finalized
You must be still so you can no longer terrorize
Cries of atrocity and injust on humanity as you disguise
As you take your last breath
It will be my duty to escort your ass to the next lifetime
Bye, Bye!
Motherfucker Buddha Bless
Peace Be Still
Amitabha

A Telepathic Message

Chicago June 2007

as I look to the east
I call out to my spiritual guide
a Shaolin Priest
he becomes the only one I can confide in
since my blood father became deceased

teach me teacher
teach me the ways of the world
teach me how to defend myself as
the wicked spin, weave and twirl their negative
trying to disrupt the ascension of this black pearl
sink this ship many would attempt
I shall prevail though bruised
from the smoldering fire I appear with a limp

Shifu
you told me "Always love yourself"
so I stay clear of those who would try to dim my light
trying to determine my wealth
I bare the marks on my heart
from remarks and arrows shot in the dark

like you, my teacher
I am considered a rebel!
they choose to try to put us down because
they can't reach this level of mastery

hoping to disrupt the chi flow
as I look to the east, the sun begins to cast it's early morning glow
the rise of this glorious fire ball!
in my moments of desperation, I must make another call
telepathic messages across these miles
it is I Shifu, your disciple child
amitoufo

When I Die

Chicago June 17th 2007

when I die
I hope to have completed my mission
when I look to the heavens and listen
I hear God giving me permission
to heal souls and broken hearts
tattered spirits who's eyes can no longer see in the dark
will the sun shine brightly or torrential rains fall to again float Noah's Ark?
he said "You my son must be willing to do your part
be my messenger to the ones who cannot hear
tell them life is to be lived not feared
help the child with support and cheers
dry the eyes that shed such sorrowful tears"
he said "To many, your powers may seem to peak at a limit
only because they walk through life unsure and timid
teach them to believe in the word known as karma
I don't care if they're Christians, Jews, Muslims or
if they study the Dharma"
yes my Lord, I shall do my best!
I must hurry cause I can hear the clock counting down as it tics in my chest
may I utter the word "Love" as I take my last breath!
may we all recognize that life is a challenge and to live is the test
from day one, I've been battling against the wicked
without a moment of rest
rest when you die!
breathe deeply to force the negative around you deep into your lungs
when you exhale, may it purify the next mans breath so
no wickedness will fall from his tongue
the air is sometimes stale from aged old garlic
someone must step forward
someone must start this awakening
there will be more turmoil before it brings peace
God whispered in my ear that he will not let me become deceased
until my work is complete!
from an adjective came a positive
from the adverb I gave my solemn word!
to the brink of hell I must be willing to change that word to a noun
when completeness is found
that's when the father will allow me to come and wear the crown

when I die
I wish to be cremated and my ashes be spread around the world
so as man takes that breath before committing an unthinkable act
through the nose I shall enter and go straight to the back of his dome
reprogram his cortex telling him defend but not to attack!
when I die
I'm gone fly!
The Messenger
peace love wisdom

The Landing Gear Is Jammed

Chicago January 1, 2012

Ride 'em space Cowboy!
Man
I'm an absolute genius!
Overstand I mean this in a most sincere way
I finally learned how to breathe to maintain homeostasis
As a disciple of Shaolin I gotta go places deeper
Deeper into the third eye
Stacking them vertebrae's of the spine so
I can touch the sky and blow a kiss into the wind
Fly high!
Where the birds would hover
Where molecular structures of precipitation form to make you run for cover
In a down pour!
We 'bout to rock this mic for sure!
Come on board
Flying so high
Touch the friendly skies
Huh
Captain the landing gear is jammed
We gone flip the switch and if it don't work
We coming in like the 69 Drunken Monks from Shaolin
Huh
Captain the landing gear is jammed
We gone flip the switch and if it don't work
We coming in like the 69 Drunkard Monks from Shaolin

Except I'm coming crashing in to my own dome
I wanna make sure there's always somebody there at home
Even if I'm alone but never by myself
Traces of cosmic dust do I puff from the Orion Belt
There I converse with God who hovered in a stealth
Then an image of Jesus was shown
Shalom!
Turning seltzer water into wine
On that day it was forbidden to eat the swine

Allah's image became so divine
That's when my mind froze in that moment in time
Like the Buddha In deep meditation
Flying through the skies in paralleled alternate galaxies is my destination

Huh
Captain the landing gear is jammed
We gone flip the switch and if it don't work
We coming in like the 69 Drunken Monks from Shaolin
Huh
Captain the landing gear is jammed
We gone flip the switch and if it don't work
We coming in like the 69 Drunkard Monks from Shaolin

Now I understand the essence of Tai Chi
As the solar Systems collide to form yet another galaxy
In Wing Chun we bridge the gap
Careful not to be too rigid or you just might snap
Like the vines on the tree
Recognize this circular energy that drips all your precious sap
Like blood and bones
Spread your wings and flow back home cause
It don't matter if the landing gear stays in retract

Huh
Captain the landing gear is jammed
We gone flip the switch and if it don't work
We coming in like the 69 Drunken Monks from Shaolin
Huh
Captain the landing gear is jammed
We gone flip the switch and if it don't work
We coming in like the 69 Drunkard Monks from Shaolin

Accept…

Peace Love Wisdom

The Edict...Year of The Horse

01.22.09 Chicago

Like the lone horseman, I travel these snowcapped miles
802 to be exact and for you Shifu, I bring the gift of a smile
From my heart
Last time I shared a piece called "As I Emerge from the Dark Into the Light"
Tonight I want to share with you something and give it with all of my might!
You shared with me over the wires some insight
When I confessed that every now and then I would light up and
Inhale of the meditative weed
While others would judge
you shared words only a true Buddha would breathe
you simply said "Don't stop expressing yourself" and
With those words, my pen continues to bleed!
Though I don't inhale of the chalice anymore
I give thanks to the Buddha for training me to walk through the doors!
So as your disciple, I have become a messenger!
To all my Shaolin brothers and sisters
know that it is time to step forward and pass on the teachings so divine! but
Remember to watch your back
Wickedness does exist and is in constant attack!

My chant becomes simple
from the physical came this mental
I now dwell in the spiritual

Last Call

Amitabha
Here is a moment of decision
I'm being given an opportunity to pursue a dream but
it must be done with absolute precision
if not I could forever be imprisoned in this empty shell
you can always tell by the way shit smells
if it's gonna be a long and rocky road or
if the shit is fertilizing an actual Zen garden
you just might overstand why your life was as it was way back then
While everyone else would only pretend
you must overstand
the only way to get you there within that dream realm
you must look deeper
as the messages pass before you in a transparent film
Like in life we must go forward
like the camera that fast forwards or
press the button for speed rewind
to help remind you of something that was a powerful ripple in time
I say this because we're all here as pieces of the universe
Taking into your pores matter
as it circulates throughout the atmosphere into the multiverse
where the meteors and asteroids disperse
like the blood cells that run through your veins
from your head to your toes do the bloodlines stream
maybe the black hole is actually the belly of a beast and
we're nothing more than parasites living as he lay there deceased
somehow this blue-green planet still survives
this becomes the contemplation
why am I still alive?
So much shit happens in a millionth of a second
In the blink of an eye déjà vu will always keep you second-guessing
Should you open your heart like the Buddha or hire bodyguards for protection
Every step you take in this journey leaves an impression
Either as a martyr or as a scholar
Teaching life long lessons
forward is the direction that I choose

push a little harder because there's not a moment to lose
Life is too short but just maybe long enough to pursue
Before the last call is song out and life as we know it is through
Last Call…
Amitabha

Don't Kill the Messenger

Chicago 2011

Am I my brothers keeper?

Gotta stay on point cause the night cloaks nocturnal creepers

Many fall victim to the sleepers hold

Struggling for air to breathe in through the nose

Your limbs have stiffened and gone cold

Suffocating by this disease called crime

Laid out as a model for another chalk line

If you're not careful, these times can pollute your mind

Homie points a pistol at your head and says "What's yours is mine!"

Tells you he's the mastermind of your worst nightmare

Says he wants to cap your ass

hoping to scare you into pissing into your pants

The worlds a beast and she summons you to dance

This is the real deal not no Harlequin Romance in France

Can't crack under pressure cause this would be his pleasure

At an arms length would be a coincidental measure

Before the bullet falls into the chamber

Might I be able to sever his throat?

I always keep my blade hidden or cloaked

Don't let the silver in my coat fool you

I went to the same academia that schooled you

Worldwide they call it the streets but

Where I from they called it the hood

That preyed on the retched and the dumb

To some, we were worthless as scum

Tonight will be the night you picked on the wrong one!

Am I my brother's keeper?

Through his eye's I became the soul peeper!

Like the words going right over your head

I've been trained by my Shaolin Teacher

The drunken mantis master who taught me to see deeper

He said the hesitations will give me a chance

The world is a beast and upgrades your dance!

I put him in a trance

I hypnotized this man with the wave of my hands

His blood now runs off my blade and as it hits the ground it turns to sand

When he looks upon me, he utters with fear, "Sand Man"

My spring steal returns to be cloaked by my waistband

I looked into the full moon and said, "They call me Chan Man"
Like Spider Man my senses are beginning to tingle
Again I must go deeper to mingle to place underground
A secret place for grunts and messengers and

there I found
This brother who could be identified by the sound
As the granddaddy clock bell would ring
J Bell made that horn sing!
He gave me sanctuary from the demons
who would battle on the upper ground
Hoping to gain control of an underground haven called the North Pole
Controlled breaths blown into the mouthpiece
Sound reminds me of an earlier time when life was sweet
Play that beat! play beat!
Soon I'll be back up on my feet
Cause I must return to the streets
With a message that I must deliver
To those who take advantage of the weak
To those who constantly reach with a palm stretched out and
Handouts are all they seek!
Don't kill the Messenger was the law whispered through the land
Who is this diabolical radical trying to seize the pen from my hand?
With this pen as my sword
I've trekked over mountaintops and across ocean floors
Through the rippled currents I've sailed!
You sent your dog soldiers through the deepest seas
Wanting to take the wind out my sails
By the power of this pen, the truth shall prevail
So came the storms that would put out the fires of hell!
Towering waves cascading over like giant melted glaciers
I washed ashore like shredded drenched paper
The Night Watchmen asked me if the stories were all true or
If they were nothing but tall tales?
He said the Kraken was given a contract for this messengers head
Thank God he failed!
This Message must reach the Mediterranean
Where Sinbad the Sailor sailed
A secret map that led me to this drinking well
Let that bell ring!
Let that bell sing!
Don't kill the messenger cause there's important news he brings!
The clock began to chime while Bell played that song

While Morse Code signals were being translated
Through the ding and the dong!
Welcome to the liberation became more than a song
We 'bout to right some wrongs!
Am I my brother's keeper?
Like the 72 Chambers of Shaolin Temple
It's time to go deeper!
Play that beat, play that beat!
Am I my brother's keeper?
Nia's Cafe

Peace Wisdom

Loud and Clear

Chicago 1999

black man
don't you understand your advances towards me are all in vain
regardless of your intent, my feelings remain the same
even as a friend, I refuse to try
I don't care if it's a shoulder you want to lay your head on and cry
we are of separate worlds and totally different views
I care not to know your name or walk in your black shoes
so do me a favor and just leave me alone
you'd probably have a better chance if you would stay with your own!

Sincerely
closed minded

Oh My Sweet Lord

Chicago December 31 2011- January 1 2012
Stroke of Midnight

It's time to cast in a new year
Let go of yesterdays fears
Respect to the Most High for creating the stratospheres
So I can breathe
Conscious of the atoms creating me and my being
I overstand why I'm constantly seeing these grooves you keep putting into my dome
So smooth!
My God, you know how to groove!
This would be the day you decided to come and chill with me
He said, "My son, with me, be still thee
For I grant ye yet another day to translate the sacred dome of my split personality"
He said, "Play, play this beat and spit it strong!
For outside your door there's a lot that might seem wrong
Within each and every person plays a song
Play your song and once you're connected
You'll forever be protected
But you gotta go deep!
Deep into that subconscious, there you gone find me
And you shall seek
Consciousness!
A real sense of my existence!
Fo Flight Play that beat
Come on up into the stratospheres and come hover with me!"
Oh lord, I gotta go and meditate
Deep into my soul so I can escape
This manmade rat race
Trying to disconnect me from my higher self
From you my lord, from you
They cannot disconnect me from you
No one can disconnect me from you my sweet lord

Cause Sweet Lord
I know you exist
The name man gives you, I know don't even make the galaxies top list
Of your real name
Cause it's a shame we don't recognize that the answer
is imbedded within our own brains

Within this matrix it becomes a consciousness of every woman and man
To know this higher self
Is the inner wealth
That stretches into the galaxies where you play your lute and
the sound of your guitar and a flute
Creating this rhythm of your solar systems circular spin as its felt
God blow that wind and send it into the next cycles inevitable end
Oh lord, I gotta go and meditate
Meditate
Deep into my soul so I can escape
This manmade rat race
Trying to disconnect me from my higher self
From you my lord, from you
They cannot disconnect me from you
No, no, no, no one can disconnect me from you my sweet lord
Cause disconnecting me from you is disconnecting me from me
Disconnecting you from me is disconnecting me from we and
This will never be!
Oh my Sweet Lord

Peace Love and Wisdom

69 Dragons Spitting Into The Sun

Chicago February 2011

Fo Flight
"Focus on your breathing"
Shifu said, you must focus on your breathing
Fo-cus"
I've been given a gift to spit
Spitting that real shit that comes from the belly of your soul
For whatever reason my Shifu gave me the sacred Shaolin Scroll
Maybe that's why he named me Heng Fo
It was time to take control of myself
He said, "Open up your heart sutra first
This shall decrease the thirst for the coin filled purse"
With the scroll I found my inner worth
In ancient Chinese character I must develop and it starts in the dirt!
So it's time to grow
It's time to train
Grow into your name
Now fly into the wind
Spin like the 69 dragons spine while they ascend into the sun
Spitting them lyrics!
Don't you ever quit it!
Now focus on your breathing
Never stop believing
That you are the greatest of all the stars
That stretches into the farthest galaxies
See your gift to spit!
Now breathe them 69 dragons

Spit it into the sun!
69 Dragons and Tigers Fist are about to have some fun!

If you don't wanna get burned I'd suggest you start to run!
Leaping Leopards chose your weapons
69 Dragons is spitting into this microphone cause
he's ready to take on MEGATRON
King Kong
Godzilla
Babylon
With the infamous technique from USA Shaolin Temple

called Snake Spits its Tongue
SOUND THE ALARM
SOMEBOBY BEAT ON THE DRUM!
Here they come, Here they come

The Dragons are coming!
The Dragons are coming!!!
Humming this melody
Wings flapping
Blazing fireballs zapping
Tails cracking while I'm snapping on every microphone that stands before we
Getting hooked into this electricity
69 Dragons spitting the essence of my soul
sweet lord we 'bouts to lose control
69 Dragons Spitting into the Sun
Spit that Shit!
I'm a Poet!

Peace Love Wisdom

Thug Passion

Chicago June 2007

I might not have that thug passion but
I sho 'nuf can leaving you asking
who was that masked man?
around the world they simply know me as Heng Fo
from the ChanClan!
I'm the man who's gone keep this real smooth
make you wanna groove to this beat
now that I got you on your feet
let's take it to the streets
so those who don't know
will come to see
I've been anointed by the Most High
If you're not hating then
show me some love as I pass by!
there's always that one who wants to exchange some blows
instead of seeing deeper into the messages
he wants to be my foe
here we go!
here we begin to grow
my heart secretes temple love
wanting to share some wisdom with the young bloods
here came another moment preconceived
when karma gives its next lesson
who gone believe?
it's not in my genes to show up and deceive
I am who I say I am

I don't give a damn! cause
where there's one who won't
there is another who will
that shall be the one who wants to feel
life is a giant workshop where we should try to enhance these skills
to deal with life, you have to be equipped
some choose to walk the path of Bloods and Crypts
Vice Lords who have lost their grip
I became a disciple but didn't have to get jumped in!

the doors were wide open and Shifu let me begin
I made a vow as well and was excepted
I gave myself to the temple of Shaolin!
here's my thug passion
that's created a chain reaction!
we don't have to go out gay bashing or
participate in talk trashing others
robbing and killing innocent soon to be mothers
scholastic brothers
cops undercover or
lovers as they embrace longing to discover!
true romance gives all living things a chance
I might not have that thug passion but
I'm willing to dance and
give you all of me!
the question is
which side do you wanna see?
I too came from the hood
I'd be dead by now if I would have
that's why I got big calves
I chose to walk, no run!
from what would be a destructive path
alas!
I know who and what I am
I give myself the needed love so
it's easy to shrug all the unnecessary off my back
Shifu said you must be willing in life to attack
as a disciple
I stay on track and
give you some of this thug passion!

peace love ❧ wisdom

No Need

...Thoughts Chicago may 2007

no need in preaching if the teachings you forgot
back in the days we were shot down with rocks
Jesus said while he was nailed on the cross
that's where truly his story was to be told and never to be lost
'forgive them father for they know not what they do'
when I finally die
I'll be with you
then there'll be
no need in bragging about how many chains I got
no need in bragging about how many been shot
I'm a Shaolin disciple so
I don't carry a glock
no need in bragging about how many bullets I've stopped
no need in banging on the block
no need for that little girl getting knocked up
no need in getting those 23 inch rims
no need in acting like a gangster who only pretends
no need in calling them bitches and hoe's if I ain't their pimp
no need in being on the top 10 most wanted list of a corrupt government
no need in having a shootout with them crooked cops
this my brothers has got to stop!
there's just no need
no need
that brother started to bleed
fell onto his left shattered knee
placed in cuffs

watch your back before somebody try to rape your butt
no need to have to hang on this block
no need in not giving life all you got!
no need in disrespecting my mom
no need in calling every educated black man uncle tom
no need in babies starving from crumbs
no need in suicide romancers and their suicide bombs
no need in fighting in a war
Bush ain't worth me dying for
no need for swastikas painted on Synagogue doors

ain't nothing wrong with getting paid to mop up floors
no need in being in the windy city if you're shy
this town will beat you down then leave you to die
no need to sit there and cry
dust yourself off like a soldier
no need in asking why? why? why? why?
no need in stereotyping me cause of my kinky hair and tattoos
no need in acting like you know me
if you've never walked in my shoes
that would be like saying you like B.B. King yet
you never listened to the Blues
no need in getting turned out by them processed and pharmaceutical drugs
no need in giving if it ain't with love
no need in speaking if it ain't the truth
I'd rather clinch my teeth and fire off from my wisdom tooth
no need in giving if it ain't with all you got
if you wanna be in this circle
you gotta wanna take it to the top!
if not
no need in being with the North Pole Crew
when Bell drops the beat
you gotta know what to do!
no need in listening if you ain't trying to hear
me, Deuce and Bell got some sweet something's to whisper in your ear
if you fear?
well
we trying to share some ancient wisdom called chi
from our hearts flow black diamonds and pearls of absolute pure energy
if you're still having a problem feeling this flow
come to North Pole's Dojo
where your first lesson little grasshopper
will be to take it slow!
then you'll come to know
open your eyes and realize
the sky is limitless!
Infinite…
Peace Love Wisdom

Welcome To The Temple Hall

NY Feb. 2007
U.S.A Shaolin Temple

Welcome to the temple hall
wulong ziaozhu (black dragon coils around pillar)
ascends to the top of the wall
as the Abbot calls out the next movement
I stand in line with 60 strong seeking improvement
guided by a spirit who is truly heaven sent
how fortunate for us that this Buddha fled a suppressing government
that tried to tame and control the Dragon
It might not be right but this is where I begin bragging
Shi Yan Ming is my Shifu
ever since I met this man
many think I'm a cave dwelling dork
the three wells taste like the fourth
sweeter and sweeter life has become
I watched my father take his last breath not too long ago
I no longer feel naive or dumb
I too saw the light while he levitated with the sun
I'm sure it was his spirit who helped me write the epic piece
"Put Down Your Guns!"
listen to the heart beat like the talking drums
pulsating within the walls of my chest
Shifu taught me how to bounce the negative stuff from my chest
as if I were wearing a bulletproof vest
the slugs have left many battle marks
believe in the Buddha so these rounds fired off will never pierce your heart

I was torn apart because
here is home! I didn't want to leave
my brothers and sisters all struggle within themselves
look into the eyes of Shifu, how quickly he can tell
where your soul and heart dwells and
without fail, if your heart is flat
to Shifu and these temple hall walls, I pledge a vow
I'll be back!
in fact Shifu, I'm never leaving cause

when I'm back in Chicago, the chi you've shared
gives me reason to keep on breathing
for as long as I can!

until the Dharma transcends my soul and
this physical becomes granules of sand
in the hour glass
I read the message written within the sand granule
it simply read
that it was time to return to class
I need to bare down and return to this beautiful pain
accept the fact that these poetic strains promote such a profound change
I have embraced you, Shifu so many centuries ago hoping to be trained!
maybe that's why you gave me my name
first you named me Monkey
because of...? I don't know why, honestly
it was too strange because that was my secret ninja assassin name
that only I and Buddha knew
as I grew in the temple, I guess it was quite simple
you knew when I would become cerebral
others mistake my antics as being a bit mental
with confidence
you named me Shi Heng Fo
I kneel before you
thanking you!
may I take a moment to kiss the temple floor
Thank you Shifu
for welcoming me through the temple doors!

Amitoufo Amitoufo Amitoufo

The Messengers Journey Continues...

Chicago June 2007

who told you this was gonna be easy?
sometimes it feels like an incredible ride and
then it can feel nasty and sleazy
the underground is much more peaceful than what lies on the surface
if you're to survive this life
you'd better be prepared to join the circus
pay special attention to the poet who recites words of wisdom in verses
he is also a Tai Ji master so the lessons learned will serve you purpose
watch how he breathes as his posture bends in the wind
opening up what he calls the Sacred Passages of the DanTien
he said you must be able to calm and relax the mind
find your spirit self then leave the physical world behind
here is where the answer of every question would combined
with another truth confirming what has been sought since
the beginning of your time
it is said that every form that you learn and
every step taken will retrace and guide you back to your starting place

allow the wind to be your compass when you can no longer see straight
whether you're blinded by time or from drinking aged old wine
some of these movements are mimicking
creatures dancing to the sound of wind chimes
the moment you're told not to move
it would behoove you to listen and pay attention
that very moment could cost you your life
there's a tale of a spirit that kills every other night
you can't see him when he's coming but you can feel the blade of his knife
the master said if you are clear and precise
you will cast a vibration off the ghost's blade
this will protect your soul and keep you alive!
the final lesson taught was The Nine Steps To The Impregnable Gate
master this movement because it shall determine your fate!
each step must vibrate the earth while you wield your sword to penetrate
at that moment when the blade pierces his heart
it is essential to look away!
one stare into his transitional glare will turn you into stone
at that very second when he takes his last breath
you must burn him to the bone!
this will ensure he never returns seeking vengeance against the holy
once more the master instructs but this time with more chi!
we cannot be merciful to this demon so

it will not be enough to bring him to his knees
if he is victorious
then your soul will belong to he!
this we cannot allow to be
with that said
the master said you are dismissed to continue this journey!
may the Buddha forever watch over thee
while crossing the desert
there is a place you can rest your head if you are weary
many wanderers and transients pass through so here be cautious and leery
Dragons Inn is the den that hosts some of its own hidden acts of horror
lets just say don't eat the meat or you'll drop to your knees
cursing the floor while reciting the Torah as
your intestines bleed not knowing
you've just ingested human flesh and feces
in this barbaric land, man is only subspecies
the Geisha girl is staring
be careful of her glares
as sweet as she looks, I assure you she's not what she appears

if you turn your back on her without caution
her motives will become quite clear
this is not the place to make friends so
one slip, you will die and no one will be heedful
she can be quite seductive in enticing you
to want to give her pleasures
if you can stay on guard while experiencing her touch and
womanly treasure
enjoy the fruit!
because this could be the only time you'll ever know such feminine lips
the pearl juice that oozes from in between her southern hemisphere drips
it will intoxicate you so be heedful of how much you sip
four days would pass before you awaken from the hypnotic dip
it could only be fate that she would fall in love with you that first night
that's why shy couldn't slit your throat when
the moment would have been just right
I guess it is possible to make friends in such a faithless place
as companions, these messengers continue to trek the earth
continuing on this quest for the place where truth is birthed
to make sure the message never reaches its destination
a bounty has been offered
you have now tripled in worth
dead... watch your back!

Children Learn What They Live

Chicago June 2007

Children truly learn what they live
teach them hate and discontent
they soon become property of the government
why does that brother have a gun in his hand?
what is it about death he don't seem to understand?
Children learn what they live
too many days with a joystick in hand testing his reflex
the unthinkable actions shall forever perplex
television takes the place of mom and dad
leaving negative impressions in the child's head
so sad you stand there stunned insisting
nope, not my baby!
you'll wish you had
taught her that even in a life of misfortune
we should give thanks to God and be glad
that we can share another moment in time
crimes done by hands never to know the meditative feel
while polishing your shoes to an absolute shine
another one lost now has to serve a lifetime sentence for a crime
Children learn what they live
inspired by moments of neglect and sexual abuse
only hand to console the child is the very hand
that helped to set the demons loose
this is what the child has lived
if no one intervenes, in future this is what they too will give
to another child who also shall learn to live while being a sieve
soaking up all the knowledge from this professor
before the sand in the hour glass fills and
he begins to undress her
lord bless him and her
raping her body that houses a soul already bruised
how did the devil get so lucky
he's deflowered more than Chucky Cheese could seat
a mission not so Impossible
this was yet another who thought it was possible
to dismantle families and shatter its core
another learned lesson for an innocent child
take a second look deeper when you see her smile

what lesson did she learn?
why can't little Bobby come out and play?
you want to know what he has learned
ask him a question and let's see what he gone say

he might know where uncle Ron's gun is or
Uncle Joe hid his stash in the mattress in the baby's crib
how does the child know this so well?
through whispered words and body language, they can tell
this is we
teaching them to die or to live
steal or to give?
should be a rhetorical question
why is there a moment of contemplation?
that shouldn't be relative to a good life no matter the situation
if the child learns consciousness
no negative shall absorb to make him become weakened to the suggestive

children learn what we give
let's give them hope for a future so their children might relive
our happiness as bearers of love and the nutrients of mother earth
she is grand guardian of mankind
teach the child we progress faster when combined
higher when we also inspire
another to push himself into levels once thought impossible
this would be my version of teaching a child the gospel
help to remove some of the hostile
behavior is learned then interpreted
to an impression of this lesson
taught by another with no parenting skills
if you've raised a human machine that kills
and kills with no regret
chances are he might be out paying mama's and papa's bets and debts
children learn what they live!

wisdom

The Seed

Chicago 2006

an innocent spirit
as pure as the moon and sun
you've changed my life
since the day you were born

I would whisper words to you
while you slept in your mama's womb
I remember you telling me one night
"daddy, I'll see you real soon"

the day you came
there wasn't a cloud in the sky
for it was that day in the heavens
when all the angels spread their wings while they cried
their tears fell because of a wonderful creation
God crafted a golden child and sent her to this world to make preparation
another angel on earth to heal those in need

how amazing you healed Carol the day you planted the seeds
you and that smile!
such a nurturing being fast forwarded in time
your eyes have seen so many things from past lives
maybe that explains your fascination and dream like state
whenever you hear wind chimes

how amazing it is to watch you grow
if I should die before your conscious years
through these journals you will come to know
me
your father
you?
Jamaica Blu
Soon you will come to know just how much I truly love you
the seed...
my seed!

Daddy's Little Girl

Chicago 2007

standing here waiting in time while daddy's gone
I promise you baby, daddy won't be gone too long
I'm sorry for having to be away from you
I promise you baby, I'm putting my heart into
every possible avenue to see us through
I promise you baby, if you believe in me
these efforts shall give you a better clue
I want you to know where you come from
so my journey has begun
my sweet baby
right now you're too young
for now
travel through these pages

there she stands in black and white
waiting for daddy to come pick her up tonight
don't worry baby, daddy won't miss his flight
tonight, I'm gonna show you the time of your life!
I promise you baby cause I really miss your smile
I hope you know how proud I am of you being my beautiful child
when is the last time I told you that
I love you!?!
I truly do

Love Wisdom Peace

Is It the Hood or The Ghetto?

Chicago 2007

here I walk through Cabrini Green
all bare the marks of tainted dreams
brother approaches me and asks what am I doing?
while I capture images of vacant buildings where death is still brewing
five-O searching each building cause somebody called it in
there's a dead body laid out somewhere said the informant
it wasn't a murder cause there wouldn't have been a call
chances are this was an overdose of someone chasing the 8 ball or
tainted crack that put this one dead on his back
that was probably the best hit he ever had
that puff got you out of the hood slowly but fast!
no need in worrying about who gone get the next bag
I see the kids walking around like nothing happened
as I stand here talking to the shorty's
I realize one of these boys might be packing!
I shall show no fear
the ghetto that I came from is not too far from here!
I asked a little brother who couldn't be more than 12 years old
"Can I ask you a question?"
each looked me dead in the eyes and said
"Not with that camera on!"
though they were kids, these little soldiers were grown
though the buildings are all almost boarded up
this is still their home and
as a soldier would, they defend it cause this is what they know
something tells me they knew something about that body strewn out on the floor
no doubt they just happen to pass it by while on their way out to play some ball
one felt I might be trying to stall
he thinks I'm five-O!
"I ain't here to disrespect you
I'm just like you, I grew in the hood too
Ida B Wells"
I don't have any bullet holes or track marks to add to the story I would tell
well, they just took off!
one looks back and said "No disrespect to you!"
I wish I had that cd on me to give them a deeper clue
one young brother asked me if I rapped?
I told him about the piece "Put Down Your Guns?

I recited the first verse before these homies took off and to run
not necessarily away from me
this is life for them in the ghetto
if you've not lived under these conditions then your third eye could never see

this is there Iraq and Gaza Strip!
brothers got to stay on point and not trip
over a fallen soldier who got hit so the rest of the journey he can't make
one shorty said it's the same shit going on though
in a majority of the buildings, the tenants had to vacate
these kids have been forced to grow faster so they might survive
it's not uncommon for bullets to rain from the sky!
they're told to believe in something and have a bit of faith
that's easier for an outsider who has never been to the hood and faced
the girls must stay in groups so the crackheads won't try to rape
bars covering windows and fenced in walkways so they can't escape
Cabrini is definitely the ghetto
at one point there use to be Good Times
J.J use to call himself "Kid Dynamite" with his verses and rhymes
these verses still ring out
some of these lyrics seem harsh to those who were given a better route
Kid Dynamite is right
shells filled with gunpowder to help them fight each other
the innocent run for cover
the bangers bang as the gunshots ring
another dead child discovered
these homies are soldiers and do not cower!
I look to them as beautiful ghetto flowers
who could use some of that money that has been funding wars abroad
we have to show them love before
they turn to the true dark side and become outlaws!
the hood is a community of separate houses and apartments
the ghetto has them living on top of each other like there living in prisons
likened conditions to the way we were stacked into the slave ships or
as if we were living in a department store
yeah, they refer to each other as nigga's, bitches and whores
I mean hoes
this life ain't easy!
condo's being built to encase them even deeper into the trenches by these sleazy
politician's who shake hands with the masses
I wonder if he's ever been to Hudson St. where the grass is rarely green
I can only imagine what this majestic tree has felt, heard and seen
learn how to handle a ball or tumble to the gangster rap call

if no one helps, like the buildings they will fall
victim to an environment that burned these souls to the 3rd degree
their exterior has in its own way been boarded up
so no one is allowed to see
instead of their souls you see a community
that appears to be out of control
if our city chiefs would only recognize these are smoke signals
from descendants of brutality who are trying to
communicate the best way they can
no one has threatened to
close down Columbine but

to remind us of a tragedy, there's a memorial each year
no one is being reminded of the shedding of blood and tears
for these misfortunes, someone's spending a fortune!
to get these people to keep on torching the very place they live
with no one wanting to give
at least some respect
in the hood
that's all you own!
the way the youth have grown
even that's gone
the elders aren't looked at as the wise
they are considered the old and feeble ones who have lost their ties
they are blamed for leaving this generation in this mess
five-O showed up again wearing bullet proof vests
here I stand shielded by a camera and a t-shirt
if a bullet has my name on it today
that shit is going to hurt but
I choose to stand here and take in this moment
may these words add to the components to
shed some light on a situation that deserves positive view
I reach out to President Obama, Oprah, Jesse Jackson Sr. and
every other politician and I ask, "What can we do?"
there are ghetto's all over the world that need some special attention
here just happens to be a place in our own backyard no one cares to mention!
If you've never grown up in the hood or the ghetto then
these words won't make a dent
the hood and ghetto are one in the same
just structures changed
if there is love in your heart, lets help them regain
peace love wisdom

Conscious Sentinel

by Matty David aka Mama Love
L.A. to Chicago 2007

to todays youth
50 and under
he that hath an eye
let him read it
I have a responsibility and
you say, my message being?
there is non greater
than the I Am
there is a fountain of youth within you and
It's called love
those you cast aside in indifference and ignorance
there is a universal law
it's called Elimination!
in this process
I perceive it is the universal way of deleting
unneeded info or input
however
you must beware of the things
people and circumstances you eliminate
know the truth
when you hear it
store it!
eliminate negativity which is garbage
to make room for nothing but truth
become wealthy!

and all else will come to you
peace
love
wisdom

Bang! Bang!

Chicago July 13th 2007

Another youth shot dead
somebody put a bullet in his head
cause of something he would say
he simply said he ain't in that gang!
he wanted to put his mind to better use
instead of playing your hood games
Bang! Bang!
he strains trying not to fall
in life he heard a better call
he might be that next B-Ball Superstar
you take his future into your hands cause
you don't want to go far!
drive by in them old school cars
that boy had a G P A of 4.0
everybody in his family would come to know
he was gonna become a professor of mathematics
unfortunately, he could figure out how to dodge
them bullets from your semi automatics
riddled with bullets at close range
the funeral has to be a closed casket
Bang! Bang!
with y'all, he don't wanna hang
he wants to step away from the block
not just cause somebody needs to cop
some rocks or weed or just to make another bleed
why he gotta bleed cause you would concede?
Willie Lynch said he'd teach us fear, distrust and bare envy
against our own so we continue this indoctrination
keep oppressed this black nation!
they sit in patience while you blaze another down
because of his determination clashing with your starvation for life
you do the bidding for every slave master by continuing the killing
taught for generations within every plantation since at least 1772
you think your hood is poor?
it's wealthy with alcohol, drugs and gun
wake up man!

they're giving them to you!

just like the Muslims, Africans and Columbians
every freedom fighter or militia fighting for a cause
man you gotta hit that button to pause
it's raining bullets and as always
mystery Babylon is trying to play Santa Claus
knowing you'll enjoy the new toys
see how the Africans rape and kill
they indoctrinate their little boys
now new soldiers to continue this genocide employed some centuries ago
no troops sent to help cause this is the hidden blow
by a man who recognizes the riches of Mother Africa and
this is his best way to secretly take control
of land so rich in oil, minerals, diamonds and exotic creatures
with such atrocities
you'd think it would become the main feature on the news
constant blood shed and a disease the world has come to dread
babies starving cause they've not been fed
Bang! Bang!
still no funds available to help you out yet
enough funds available to close housing projects down giving them doubt
about who you are?
a man or a nigga?
like in Africa, we walk aimlessly trying to figure
oh out of time!
cause another misguided youth committed the next premeditated crime
Bang! Bang!
who wants to ride the freedom train?
ride with me so we can reprogram the brain
recognize yours doesn't deserve this pain
that the colonials would bring and somehow maintain for centuries
these invisible shackles around our feet and hands
while the noose was never let loose
that's why we are in alarming numbers the majority in prison cells
capturing our youth so they can't be the next Fredric Douglas, Harriet Tubman,
Dr. Martin Luther King, Marcus Garvey, Malcolm X, Tiger Woods, Author Ashe,
Chris Eugene Scott, President Barack Obama
Bang! Bang!
some rose to the top but so many dead in their tracks to be stopped!
this ascension must ensue
pull your pants up over your ass man!

you've been tagged and the man is watching you
give them a reason

now you laying face down on the hood of a squad car
they say you look suspicious just cause you were sneezing
when did reaching for scotch tissue become reason for declared treason?
reached into his pocket for his cell phone
he just got blown away!
some cops are good but
them who stopped you?
man, they were members of the KKK!
I mean the United States Government
when will you realize we are descendants of
a nation that tried to absolutely annihilate or
if argued in a court of law
should get at the very least
a lifetime sentence for every century you would humiliate
using us to do your work
then prey on us like vultures
take a lesson from the Judaic culture before we completely rupture
they pay respect to those who have lost their lives
under Hitler's wicked ways
ours was worse than that
theirs because they are Jewish ours because we are black
hated because of his religion, we, because of our full body lesion
of multiple shades
wake up homies cause this happened in a sometime not so long ago days!
they say fashion comes around every so often
some of the tree's are cut down to build some of your coffins and
how often is a person of color displaced
in this case
homie became a murderer instead of a worldly defender
they smile in your face when in fact they are the pretenders
who pass bills to make sure guns, liquor and crack are in an abundance
so in the hood you will continue to kill or be killed!
what's wrong with wanting to feel
let love spill cause enough has been killed!
another carcass shoved into the casket
once plucked to put into the slave masters basket
strange fruit indeed
instead of them hanging from trees
we pick them from the ground as bloodied cotton from ghetto streets
everyone dressed alike to identify your peeps

peep this!
you just made the list as another on the cutting blocks

because of this decision
everyone one around you, especially your family
is about to hit rock bottom
you going down as fast as a slalom racer
your mama said you were so smart in school
you could have been the inventor and maker of
a new pace maker used in Olympic training
wake up brother cause the gang banging is only draining our hoods
from the next potential Oprah, Condoleezza, Colin Powell, Venus and Serena
Williams, Miles Davies, Michael Jordan, Maya Angelou, Nelson Mandela
come on fella's
this is a hell of a battle we must fight!
in order to be victorious, we must do it right
put down your guns and in the hood plant some tree's and flowers
recognize what you seek is not in the bullet but
in your mental power!
not to be fooled by those hanging on to those devices of control
help me brethren to free our ancestor's souls!
from bondage may we pay homage to peace
may the bang, bang
finally cease!
stop killing the messengers!
like the pits you breed to fight
here comes some more insight
when the canine would take a bite
have you any idea of how many gave up their lives?
if it's true about reincarnation
then each time he comes back to this generation
you blaze him to the ground!
the message goes unheard again
just as he opened his mouth to utter words about
what in meditation he had found
the only sound
Bang! Bang!
again
from your guns
you've got souls forever on the run!
brothers Put Down Your Guns!
so the elders can come forward from the ghetto's, shanty towns and favela's
these storm clouds need to dissipate and
invite in some beautiful weather
pissssst
pay attention cause they are getting clever

sending ships into outer space to eventually sever

all ties while they're hoping to find another planet to start again a colony

while we're stuck here still suffering from an economy

we'll still be here cause we couldn't afford the ticket for $2 mil!

so earth we stay while they fly off to another galaxy

gasoline costing even more

you know Bush was trying to steal some while fronting his actions with a war

bang! bang!

we gotta change!

we must unite before another mans war becomes our strain!

they've been fighting in a war for centuries

now we shall bare the tag as their forever enemy!

while our friends star trek their way through the stars

while sipping a martini

what would be some good irony

is if they ended up on the planet of the apes

based on karma

there it might suggest   that

their souls too never escape

but wait

please read this message you damn bloody apes

be careful cause they know how to persuade

that letter from Willie Lynch will teach you their wicked ways

if you don't know how

don't let them teach you how   to

bang! bang!

peace   love   wisdom

Put Down Your Guns!

Chicago 2008

either get on with living or
get on with dying
each time a gun is picked up
nine times out of ten somebody's dying defying the law or
any other who only wanted to discover
why the world is round?
how the follicles in one's hear drum identifies the sound?
hearing the rat, tat, tat of the drum skin as
the sound pulsates deep into the core of you
unlocking doors deeper than when you first recognized your awakening

Bang! Bang! Bang!

awakened by the sound of a bullet as it whizzed by her head
a piece of a hollow tip was found a few blocks down
lodged in a little baby's throat and
there she would choke on her own blood
should she die
will that little homie cry?

knowing her ambition was to know when it would be time
to begin teaching her child
how she learned to play hop scotch and four corners
taught to her by her mother
who was taught by her grandma
who was taught to by her grandfather
while she sat as a little girl on his shoulders
she just happen to bend over
now we bend over her lifeless body as mourners
put down your guns
before we lose another one!
he's got himself a Smith and Weston
the dealers not even second guessing
if this twitch needs the gun to make himself bigger or
if this red eyed devil child is an absolute nigger killer?
that's show nuf' what you called that man
before you pulled the trigger now who will consider?
there stood an even darker figure who also has been graced
by a label based on the color of his skin
again the sound enters the hear drum
depending on who says it
he's either your boy or
that nigger's scum
another round fired into the skin
now that drum can't be heard cause the bullet severed a nerve

they say twenty two shots rang out that night
little boy strapped into the car seat
six members of this family lost their lives cause
the driver lost his sight
then ran his car into a street light
pronounced dead on sight
bullet went straight through his head
fired from a gun that was held by another who has been misled
to think we must walk this journey still believing
that all we are
are
niggaz

heard on the news while held up at your boys crib for several days
there were actually seven in the ride
the little boy strapped in the car seat survived
the bullet grazed his head

ricocheted off the dash board
then caught him in the leg
that ding off his dome must have riveted with depth
doctor said he'll recover but he'll be deaf
he was the only one not to die that night
caught in a crossfire of bullets
a hail of bodies falling
to the ground nine others would fall and
drown in their own blood!
while the violence pours into the community and floods
little niggaz packing cause somebody's a grudge!
that hollow tip must have had some love cause
that little homie was blessed that day!
what were the words you would say?
that lil nigga lucky!

found you held two months later
after robbing a liquor store somewhere in Kentucky
police chief Whiteman other wise known as The Colonel said
"he likes his niggaz
I mean, chicken fried too
I told you them niggaz was wild animals and
should have been locked up in cages kept in the zoo
go get the fellas!
tell you what we gone do
we gone have us a natural old style country hanging"
from a tree became the next place this niggaz gonna be
not like on the street corners hanging, slinging rock and weed
sucking the little left out of this community
to keep the struggling off their knees

at least go Robin Hood style
you know
steal from the rich and give to the poor
to bring hope to bring love to bring respect
to bring
gun shots ring out in the middle of the day
robbing hoods of the innocent ones who never wanted to play!
gangsters, pimps and hoe's who couldn't find their way
your appointed niggaz said them niggaz got hell to pay!
A K's spray throughout the rest of the day
another niggaz lifeless on the ground and
there he lay

knowing the last words someone standing over this
almost lifeless body would commence to say
"fuck you nigga!"
from yet another brother from a different gang
niggaz don't realize
to the outside?
these niggaz all the same!
with their asses hanging out of their pants
this was the assumed posture when your great, great grand parents
received his licks from a cane
whip or the masters dick!
bare back lashes!
they weren't worthy enough to bleed where the cows would wait and graze and
be fattened up before the end of the day!
finally a chance given so
they ran away with Harriet Tubman and the run away slaves
taking days to journey to the free land
from a man who instilled a subliminal device
it now follows us to the grave
branded!
now commanded!
by this subliminal
that makes you climb the ranks of drug dealers
now a straight thugged out hardened criminal
been locked up and held down 4 times since 2009!
for crimes ranging from armed robbery to peddling dimes
bag after bag another stands in line
waiting to get another ultimate high
from a drug that literally affects your soul and
breaks your spine!
makes you go out your mind
makes you sell you own mother fucking behind!
owing the drug dealer for a quarter
now he makes you wrap your lips around him
and says "hold my water!"

like a crack head would
you sneak into his pockets
hoping to find that magical rock that fires up rockets
he slowly removes the dealers jones out
then runs home
sits back, then fires up while tripping on the couch
oh shit!

more shots rang out!

where's that nigga who stole my shit?

showed up at the front door and just unload two clips!

didn't even look to see who else was standing around

in the bedroom

sitting on the floor watching zoom

that bullet pierced her heart

mama's crying herself well into the dark cause

she knows the journey her 16 year old son will now embark!

papa ain't around to calm his little soldier down so

he's coming for revenge

got a nine and wants to unload every round in your behind

knowing he's gone end up doing time

tells his mama

"that niggaz gotta pay!"

stepped to his enemy with gat in hand and

got blazed!

the last words he would say

"that was my little sister you murdered today"

a familiar song plays in the distant

sounds like some 2Pac!

saying "niggaz are hard to kill on my block!"

a phrase that don't seem to hold much weight these days

this little homie had just graduated 8th grade

had a dream that maybe he could teach the Pitt Bulls how to behave or

maybe even become a swimmer and

dive into an Olympic pool!

man

he just wanted to finish high school!

robbing hoods of dreams because of these subliminal schemes!

I said we are

robbing hoods of dreams because of these subliminal schemes!

the Colonel and his boys are dancing in homeboys dream

found in a Motel 6, the Colonel awakens you to your screams

"get your ass up nigger! you gotta date over by the stream!"

they took him in the pitch black night

the Colonel says, "I'm sorry I forgot to read you your rights!

oooops!

where's the noose?" he asked his boys

"Who came to see another nigger swing?"

from this familiar tree that 400 years has seen generations cease

some brought their children who use this same spot to play
hide and go seek
look here little ones
this is what our grand pappy's did
got so deep into their heads they don't know who they is!
they use to be kings and warriors back in the day
exotic creatures!
look at their features
spoken in dialects of the ancients
Egypt, Morocco, Tanzania, Senegal, Madagascar
these are just a few places they're from
it took us a while to make them feel helpless and dumb
first thing we had to do was stop 'em from beating on the black skin of that drum
there is their power!
within every stroke they might find hope
can't let them feel that cause
they might revolt and
we'd have a mess on our hands
with a bunch of god damn Africans!
tie him up boys
it's time to watch this nigga swing!"
here we go again
that word nigger brings so much pain!
"Even that Seinfeld fella told you
we hang your asses upside down with a pitch fork shoved through your ass
I like him, he's got class!
he told you niggas just how he felt!
oh by the way
you won't believe where the word nigger comes from
well some of our stock came from an area called Niger
well, I must confess we couldn't pronounce it cause back then nobody got higher
than fourth grade
we heard about these Niger's being used as slaves
the Europeans and Latin's tried to teach us but
it didn't matter!
once y'all was here to stay
y'all been indoctrinated into the culture as niggers
ever since that fateful day!
amazing the power of repetition
say something often enough
now y'all rapper boys got the whole world calling you
the word everyone was scared to mention

you know, the N word!
all them civil rights movements were making us look bad
thank God for todays rap music and them do-rags and
niggaz with guns!
all we need to do is entice
make you feel inferior to us whites
now the genocide has begun
y'all scared us for a while when you picked up them pens
because of y'all, we keep a close eye on them nigger Indians!
Y'all so smart yet you can't see
it was us who shipped the weapons, drugs and disease to your front door
hell nigger
we keep you poor!
boy
y'all let us march right on in
now y'all house a majority of every county jail and state pen
writing and rapping about how them nigga's gone pay
that's what I've been trying to say!
hell nigga, you my friend
my nigga soldier!
we seek the same thing in the end
now that you know what we're about
it's time to turn your mother fucking lights out!
kill this nigga!"
Recap:
you should have put down your guns!
hear
the gun is represented by the bullet exiting the chamber and
the word you keep fire from your tongue!
until you stop blazing your brothers down
this battle will never be won
brothers
Put Down Yours Guns!
Peace Love Wisdom

Which Road Do You Choose?

Chicago 03.08.2010

Webster's definition of poetry- 1a. metrical writing; b. productions of a poet: poems; 2: writing that formulates a concentrated imaginative awareness of experiences in language chosen and arranged to create a specific emotional response through meaning, sound and rhythm 3a:something likened to poetry esp. in beauty of expression

I'm walking down a lonely road
who will I meet along the way?
I don't know
I don't know how far on this road God will let me go
sure hope I can stay on my feet
till I find my soul
will it be standing right in front of me?
again, I don't know
I'm just gonna take my time and
take it slow as I travel
talked to my brother just last Sunday
he said if you wanna live a good life
you gotta take it day by day
don't listen to what the other fools may say
they'll try to build up them road blocks
wanting to slow you down and get in your way
in life, it's ok
to stand in the pouring rain by yourself and
like a child, enjoy each raindrop while you sing and play
heard a young brother was gunned down as he was walking home
shot down by another who also is nothing but flesh and bone
how can you treat a life with such disregard?
when the rains came, did it flood your heart?
take that road?
with your soul
you'll be miles apart
soon you'll be walking alone watching your back in a penitentiary yard!
now you gotta a life time sentence to heal your battle scars
not knowing where you truly are
other than this place you know
you don't want to be
think back just before you pulled the trigger
that's when you were actually free

a member of society

though many things in the free world are definitely wrong

you could have changed the beat to the sad mundane songs

close your eyes so you can see the light

you still have an opportunity to make some of it right

instead of picking up a book

you went and got hooked and

it sho' nuf wasn't on phonics!

your mama said you use to be acute

young man's soul is now ugly and chronic

did 6th grade teach you that pneumonic device?

you picked up an instrument that now has you in a blazing gunfight!

instead of it shining bright to enhance your life

it becomes a flash that ignites a sequence of events

take responsibility for your actions my brothers and sisters

before you become permanent property of the government

who, as many have concluded, just don't care

like a slave from back in the days would sit there

on slaves ships

with that blank stare

asking, wondering why me?

what will be your destiny?

this became the ripple in time

that sparked Dr. Martin Luther King's dream!

I too have that dream

at your lowest moment you must always believe!

you have a purpose on this earth as you breathe

never stop reaching for the sky

don't stop wanting to achieve up until the last breath before you die!

even then to the heavens may you attempt to reach

why not strive to become a Doctor, a Star Watcher (Astronomer), an Olympic Diver

an Attorney, a Geologist on a worldly journey, an Archeologist,

A Metaphysicist, a Psychiatrist, an Ophthalmologist, an Herbalist

a Track Star who runs the fastest

how about an Artist who can draw the future or

a Monk who translates the Holy Sutra's

how about a Teacher

a Sunday School Preacher

a Photographer

a Poet and Book Writer?

who feels inspired by President Obama

how many of you would feel proud if Hilary Clinton or

Oprah was your mama?

there are so many roads for you to choose
some girls get tricked into having sex to make them feel loved or cool
babies having babies before graduating high school
many futures have been altered and destroyed and
left to feel like fools

no one will be able to love you more than you should love yourself
let no other determine your wealth
especially those who say you're just dreaming!
if one wants to be your friend then
they must rise to the occasion
those who tell you gangs and drugs are cool
also fell victim to the same persuasion
you see how they're behaving
killing each other and the innocent ones who were playing
now so many are afraid to try
forever waiting for something good to happen
I want to stand as a guest at your grammar school, high school and
college graduation, clapping or
at a concert where one of you were consciously rapping
to some beats to get more kids just like you
back into school and off these streets
congratulating you all on a job well done!
you are the future
which road will you choose?

Love Wisdom

Grandma Said...

in route to Las Vegas
03.22.07

they can't keep a good man down
I say they can't keep a good man down
for so long we work on them plantation
work our fingers to the bone and still
we die from starvation
how can we obtain equal opportunity
because of my sweet brown skin
there's no equality
I and I know that Jah make me strong
he gives me strength and courage to push on
to fight against those who impose injustice
we still have not truly mended the scars they engraved 400 years long
not considering that what they were doing was wrong
till this day, we try to keep our heads to the sky
use your peripheral vision to find the child who loses her way and silently cries
remember you're not alone
if you give up on faith
and turn your back on Jah
you've lost your way home
keep your eyes opened wide cause
your destiny is in your sight
these are the words my grandma said...
she said they can't keep a good man down
no they can't keep a good man down
she said stay focused cause if you can't swim

only clowns will show up at your funeral wearing an upside down frown
smiling cause you met your untimely demise
the sound of chuckles and laughter will be the only sound remnant of farewell cries of
goodbyes to those you could utter before that last sip
they will be thanking their lucky stars that your beautiful spirit is gone
step up my brothers and sisters, don't be intimidated by the foam of their lashes
tree lined streets bearing this strange fruit by the masses
careful with too much of that whole milk as
you make it through grade school classes
at least 12 ounces filled these mayonnaise looking glasses
laced with some hormones to make your bones more dense to help develop

you into a "super-igger"
create the perfect specimen then offer you a four point figure
now your time is compensated as a franchise player
pushing his chest up wanting to show some courage
cause you didn't pay attention to your education
there you stand with a bruised ego and discouraged
for over 400 years they tried and almost broke our backs
sorrowful spirits indeed
our blood makes up well over half the condensation known as the Mississippi
rivers run deep
stop shooting your brothers down by calling him a nigger
man how can you sleep?
at nightfall was when the Klan would creep and
bleed us dry!
those who would survive and bare the battle scars
while enduring mental and physical disfigurement
allowed by the figures who made up this group we call the U S Government
to the plantations we were sent
raped and beaten without consent
are these actions considered
against the law?
beaten so brutally then hung upside down
to be cut in half by men who's hearts and tongues were as jagged as a saw
grandma said you can't keep a good man down
this strange fruit had ripened long before someone cut it down
in the wind you can hear an echo rippling through time as
his lifeless body hits the ground
this sound drowns out all the laughter
as the children play around the corps
learning how to become the next slave masters
how many years and tears did our forefathers endure?
I stand before you strong and proud of who I am
that's why these words pour out from me in a manner so pure
how obscure might I be?
knowing that the blood of the Seminole also runs inside of me
why is there a warrior spirit residing within
singing incantations of a people who would not allow themselves
to sign the treaties cause they would become A Sovereign Nation
I truly believe in reincarnation cause
I've been here before!
again it was my grandma who stood at the door
with her face painted in colors representing war
saying

they can't keep a good man down
I said they can't keep a good man down!
as the blood runs through your veins
hear the sound
you are no longer lost my child
now you are found

grandma said
please teach the younger generation how to rise above the loss of hope
they're dying from these unnecessary frustrations
use the wisdom from tai ji and teach them with patience
you are their present to lead them into the future
by reminding them of the past
the spirits whisper "Don't let our death be meaningless" because
you want to go bling, bling and wear diamonds from an African blood bath
again you must recognize the correlations between life and math
I'd rather break every bone in my body and be laid up in a body cast cause
I tried to make the spirits proud
recognize the power you possess like the black cumulus clouds
let the storms begin to flow
grandma looked me straight in my eyes
before it was time for her to go
she said
they can't keep a good man down
I say they can't keep a good man down
she said
the deeper you search for truth within yourself
that's when and where you'll be found
grandma said...
wisdom

Peace and Love

Chicago Oct 1999

all I ever wanted was peace and everlasting love
such a sweet sound and so beautiful
to hold it but for a moment
subdued by its overwhelming fragrance
held captive by its simplicity
oh I'd gladly be your prisoner
tonight and every night here after
brainwash me
trickle through my veins
let me feel the rush of chasing the dragon

let the eight winds make love to my soul and
the heavens cuddle me through the night
in my darkest hour, may the angels whisper
in melodic songs filled with luscious words of sweet delight
words of love and peace

when pillows are soiled from tears of blood
may happiness overcome me
turning these tears into a sweet red wine
intoxicating those who have allowed my name
to enter their minds and fall from their lips!
It matters not on this day
I Love You All either way! -_-

peace love wisdom

Respect the Mic!

Chicago 2007

who came to bless the mic for Fo Flight?
If you're stepping up
make sure your shit is tight!
at the very least
come in peace
at the most make sure you're on point so
you don't offend the host
the host is your physical self that represents the most high
so this means we gotta keep it real and
go for absolute broke!
after the smoke clears
we gone leave some behind like four decade old toasted cheers
we are here! and
are about to rock the mic from coast to coast
we came to groove not to boast
there's enough fools out there who done gone stone loc!
watch 'em acting like slow pokes!
lyrical fireballs shot right over your head so you take me as a joke
there's always that hater in the crowd thinking he's the dopest
trying to talk over the mic
hoping he can make another lose his focus so
to you hissers, finger snappers and toe tappers
not wanting to give a kind ear and respect
to this pimped out kind of rapper
naw man, I ain't looking for adulation or a million clappers!
poetry is about sharing, caring and even sometimes swearing
if I can sit through your middle American venting
the least you can do is
hear about the life time sentencing you still keep placing on we
instead of showing love
you turn a cold shoulder like a vagabond on the streets

to a degree
we are all the same
Chicago peeps!
yeah my shits coming at you deep!
what better way to desegregate some communities then
with some spoken word poetry!

they say what you put out is what you get
so quick to judge before that first sip
I don't need to play that race card
cause you keep taking me on that trip
say my subjects are too black and tough
yeah, this groove is rough!
highly flammable lyrics ignited to scorch some butts!
cause you don't care about how the others live in such corrupt and
unfortunate circumstances that made a brother have to knuckle up!
instead of being my bredren
you want to cast me out of heaven
not hearing the echoing reverbs
like the arch angel
I come filled with action verbs, nouns
conjugated phrases and positive slurs
like a ninja
I blend in like a blur!
if you listen
you can hear this consciousness without me saying a word!
I spit out aria's, soliloquy's and sonnet's
sometimes inspired by a hit of some good chronic
it takes a brave soul to step to the center stage
prepare himself not to be dazed or fazed
to formulate and postulate ways to articulate
how to either love or hate
with debate
you sit on your ass in the audience with fear
if you were to participate
on stage is the performance and it's about to begin
I'm gone rock this beat till the very end
they say
from the womb to the tomb
respect the mic or get sucked up into this lyrical vacuum

tell them
Fo Flight69 soon come!
even tweedle dee and tweedle dumb respect the mic cause
they were having some fun!
with the beats we drop
respect the mic so
put your cell phone ringer on silence then lock or
set to vibrate
like Ron Jeremy, this money shot's all in your face or

like some sweet ear candy dripping into your ear drums
this spoken word is coming to balance out the sum of
Chicago's conscious movement
we reach not wanting to take but to make some improvements
in the hood and in the world
throw your C's up if you're grooving on these lyrical pearls!
respect the mic
or security!
escort that punk bitch out and
tell him to have a good night!

Respect the Mic!

Peace Love Wisdom

Pure Energy

Chicago January 2014

every now and then you sit back and think of where you've been
as the world continues to spin
like a spinning top that would never stop
like a galaxy exploding and hurdling out giant rocks
into this infinite space of cosmic dust
eyes fixed on so strong, you know in your gut that it's magic
from the mind of Allah, Buddha, Martin, Malcolm and even Jesus
pure energy that circles the globe
stories so old that it's impossible to believe
that these spirits were all conceived from the same seed
the one that bleeds the same blood of Adam and Eve
Atom makes me agree with Einstein's Theory of Relativity of
$E=Mc2$
don't you dare be scared of your energy that comes from way out there
I'm spinning on this great big rock
reach into myself where energy never stops!
I'm spinning on the great big rock
Reaching deep inside, energy never stops!!!
It's absolutely free!
Free energy
In this giant mass of a multiverse
why feel cursed then reach into your purse
filled with fears of who you truly are and
how simple it is to just reach in far
submerse
learn your equation of motion as you rehearse
steps of a tai ji and gung fu master
who will gladly show you the first
step into the mirror and open up the other portals to the universe
every movement made is a mathematical verse
man of color, know that you matter
gather up your dark energy
for it makes up 23% of the universes density
it's energy
be free
I'm spinning on this great big rock
reach into myself where energy never stops
can't you see?

I'm spinning on this great big rock
reaching deep inside, this energy never stops!
it's absolutely free!
It's free!
It's free, it's free, it's free consistently!
Like Bruce Lee entering the dragon and
giving out free booty whoopins'
with his nunchucks of the twin dragons rolling from the sea
to whomever is caught looking at his finger
instead of the heavenly glory
can't you see?
these same circles exists in every galaxy called you and me
the flight of the bumblebee
even the healing powers of a tree
the breath of God as he breathes into seaweed
the undeniable power of a woman and her cuchie
a beautiful black hole passed on to maintain humanity
Third eye see
I am absolute pure energy
I'm spinning on this great big rock
reaching deep inside, this energy never stops
I'm spinning on this great big rock
reaching deep inside, the energy never stops!!!

I'm spinning on this great big rock
don't stop, don't stop, don't stop!
reaching deep inside, this energy never stops
I'm spinning on this great big rock
reaching deep inside, the energy never stops!!!
I love it!
Flight Attendants, prepare for take off!
The captain has turned on the "fasten seat belt" signs
We're expecting some turbulence for this next rhyme!

Wisdom

Willis Tower

Chicago February 5, 2014

Wake up
Wake up, they're watching
Wake up, Willis Tower is watching
Skyscrapers line the distant horizon
Wealth beyond recognition while black and brown babies are dying
Streets where police sweep away any remains except for the bloodstains
No more shells found cause the weapons all came from
a classified group with a familiar name
Skyscrapers line the distant horizon
To watch this war game
The higher the floor, you're guaranteed to see more!
Scorecards kept in privatized systems
Institutions known as prisons
I hope you're still with me and I hope you're still willing to listen
Take a look at this country's old money
The Getty's, The Rockefellers, Vanderbilt's, Morgan's
How do you think the acquired all that money?
They simply took the land and territories with licenses
Created businesses while brutally massacring off the native population
Imported and sold slaves and guns
Promoting war while supplying both sides of the civil war
They controlled the politicians, the railroads and are now called "American Heroes"
Whatchu' talkin' 'bout Willis?
He rose Illinois watch tower
Once worthy to be in the book of Genus
Standing 108 and floors and can see

This giant black erection
Now owned by a Multi National Risk Advisor that makes investments
Stand on the SKYDECK with your binoculars and
You can see each and every one of these black boys getting arrested and
To be the next contestant
On the streets their skills were tested
Late night ghetto fights while sipping on refreshments
Powered by rap music, crime and a cultures depressant
A testament TO A KILLING MACHINE KNOWN AS THE GOVERNMENT
Wake Up my brothers…
Peace Wisdom Love

Who Are You?

Chicago 02.25.08

who are you to judge me?
why am I the one you're blinded by to see?
why do you envy me?
I breathe from the same mother earths breath that feeds your awaiting soul
before my face sits an empty rice bowl
granules of knowledge created in the Black Hole
upside down pyramids point into my dome
with the same eye
reflecting from my soul a mirrored image of the Buddha is shown
to the same God you declare as your own
we are shown the maps of Hieroglyphics
so specific to how the earth hurdles
through space and time of shapes like
triangles and circles, plants resonating deeper riches of the color purple
with DNA connecting us to the monkey's, dinosaur's, Pharaohs and turtles
souls so rich with red blood as it mixes blue
running through almost identical veins
who knew?
with that interchangeable mix
in almost every species she has a vagina and he has a stick
why does man tend to be a prick with tainted sperm? and
to life's fabric he ejaculates to make stick
the one missing piece to the jig saw puzzle
in plain view and your eye refuse to fix
on what is so apparent and to you painfully true
I BECOME IDENTICAL TO YOU!
who knew our fathers came from the same place
with so much mixed blood ciphered through these vessel walls
you can see in my face the culturing of ancestors
from high atop Asian mountains
fountains painted within the faces leaving more traces of
spirits who came long ago
they were drawing on the many cave wall doors and Yes!
as tall as the T Rex posses that were knocking on this caveman's door
the one's who swore if they made it out alive
they'd become lords and explorers of outer space or
as the Atlantis Underwater tribe!
told to be the lost tales of Atlantis

on the ocean floor walks my ken known as the drunken mantis
before you, I stand demonstrating how
this clan never kow towed!
we vibrated and sounds of thunder rang out loud!
guiding this to what is understood as the higher self
crawling from the depths of the ocean floor in sea floor armor we disguised
this clan that I'm bred from for another century we continue to survive
from the showers that began so long ago
taught by an aged old sage
God learned this technique, mixed with stardust and a half solar system of sunrise
when translated it's called
"when Heavenly Angels Cried"
who are you? and
who was the soul you accepted from this bribe?
talked you out of recognizing your own bloodline
through time your spirit has journeyed committing the same crime
of not knowing the only race in life is the one known as time and space
forgot when God first taught you how to meditate
in your mama's belly there you wait
to rise above the rat race
did you know you're standing in the space?
where God trekked the earth to bless this holy place!
the same God who would impregnate another flower
the one who loves white rose peddles and also loves
the late summer night drops that would for infinite hours
fertilize so the sun could then incubate
these luscious assorted buds and Lillie rugs of green would wait
from the north the wind blows carrying every drop in this torrential shower
the earth swirling from this solar systems cyclonic power
wielded by the night watchmen from the outer galactic lookout towers
all that comes from the vortex, from the far east they call it the chi flow
that's beaming through this planet putting on a symphonic light show!
connecting me to my higher self and bloodline from so long ago
within the speed of light!
my chakras are aligning with the rays piercing through the galaxies
who spoke to me the other night
who are you?
I ask this question cause it might help to define the things you do
I can't put too much time into that thought cause
if you don't know, I can't speak for you
right now the skies are blue!
blues so rich in hues you would only hear of them in a romantic fictional
soon come the rain to perform the ritual

like "I'm Singing in the Rain" Broadway musical!
I stretch my arms out wide to become host to
the beings that make up my spiritual
my mental is sharper as my ears hear the sound
light thought to have been left behind in the physical

I stand before thee knowing that we are all as one!
If you have another explanation
can you tell me? who are you? and
why from the answers do you run?
you could be the last gleam of hope for your light
in this galaxy to ever burn
I am a beacon seed fueling for my next return
a crystal of energy for a distant clansman to learn
how to connect into this spirit line to journey through the wormhole
who are you?
why do you flare that infra red at my head?
was it something that I said?
look into my eyes and see what my soul says
we were once particles scattered around the mountains
extending from the sea
the gust of air known as the Santa Anna Winds dancing to
God playing the original version to "Summer Breeze"
makes me feel so fine blowing through my mind with absolute ease!
jasmine laces the air covering up the smell of another smoking weed
ready to step out of the box
before you cast your sticks, stone and rocks
look into my eyes, I am you
you kill me, you're killing you
then the spirits that are actually here to make this queen bee spin
well, she will inevitably stop!
then mother earth will drop out of rotation
to turn the seasons immeasurably cold or volcanic hot
so many answers we could uncover before the light would go dim
fly through the ocean or through the sky, with the raindrops, go for a swim
have some tea with me as we did long ago before
another journey we would begin
is your cup half empty or filled to the rim?
again, I ask you
who are you? and
don't judge me because of this
this moment I'm having to give respect to the kiss
that filled these lungs to take me on another trip

given to you by the same spirit
filling your skeletal structure with related organs fitted into a casing of ribs
a planetary adventure within itself
look deeper inside of you
there you recognize my wealth
your balance written in the book of I-Ching
have you become possessed like Froto when he bore the ring?
like particles of debris floating through space as frozen crystals
to the far north are formed gigantic ice sickles where ice chunks trickle
glaciers filled with ice aged old clansman who have tripled
more generations of the ChanClan fall into the sea to create the next ripple

who are you is deeper than a question
it becomes the ultimate riddle
so before you put me in the middle
of something that simply requires your mental
no nonsense allowed inside the temple
he that tries to disrupt because of some temperamental
who are you not to see something so blatantly simple
we are...
the further you run in a straight line
around the earth you will circle and again find
well, You...
me swirling around within this spiraled rhyme
we either zoom by as the sight of bright or dim lights to shine
not connecting as mother earth continues to spin on a dime
while galaxies expand while waving like the dragons spine
the stars and planets all create a super space highway map and
my higher self just flew through in his stealth spaceship craft
they're able to pierce through the solar systems creating enormous gaps
he said our galaxy is a ripple in known space ocean
he felt my presence as his
while the external explodes or implodes
there matter would grow
fragmented pieces of you, of me
of we
all connecting this energy
we
you and me!
...and again the question is asked
who are you?
I am Energy
peace love wisdom

No More Mr. Nice Guy

Chicago June 16th 2007

nice try
tried to bring my spirit down
wanted me to feel knee high
what a guy!
for 15 years I've awakened at a quarter after five a.m.
prepped myself so I could be at your side
this to many is considered an ungodly hour
I showed up at your doorstep ready to help you increase your power
since that day I showed weakness for who I considered my true love
you act like I should cower and
run to the light tower and dim my lights
though you claim you want to see my name in lights so bright
it's amazing your insight
you don't care for my hair cause it's twisted too tight
under a false impression that the only women I date are white
you have only met three out of the 300 plus that have befriended me
you've become critical and blinded by what you don't see or
should I assume the hue of her skin tone will be what defines me?
to you, you say, you've found a best friend
if it's true
why do you judge me then?
It's impossible to speak of something if you don't really know
for 15 years I came loyally at your door
In that amount of time, I've cancelled only when my health was poorer than poor
getting to know you and your entire family too
I remember a conversation we had then an argument
I could tell you each and every one of their names
with my family, could you do the same? No and
this totally changed the game
instead of asking
you sat there basking in your ego
this shows how much you really want to know
remember that piece of poetry about the pedophile?
as you realized that story was about me and
how I grew up for a while as a child
I found strength in my moments of despair
You, like all the others, didn't care
you simply said with a scour on your face
"I don't care to read this"

how I felt again like the child not believed back then
you still look me in the eyes and call me your friend
ever since I brought my first manuscript over preparing for the world to see
you became so indifferent with me
since then, never did I question you when
you would have me read an encyclopedia to you while we trained
with print so small you came to know my dyslexia would be to blame
for mispronounced words and those teasers for the brain
you forgot I came to pick your wife up off the floor
remember that day when her back she would strain
I sped to her in the pouring rain
after you called me from another city
I gave you my word and showed her love not pity
now every time we meet
you try to make me feel shitty
challenging everything I'd suggest to do
If I said the skies were clouded
you'd wanna argue that they were blue
for 17 years I have yet to steer you wrong
we've been together since 1992, man!
that's a mighty long time for you to start casting doubts
you've pushed me into a corner
now I need to get the fuck out!
before you sue me like you recently suggested
that's not a phrase to be taken lightly considering all that I've invested
in my talent and wealth as a person
you've said some things I can forgive but never forget
I've given so much to you and today is my last gift!
I can no longer be your punching bag
God said choose your battles wisely so you won't be had and
I won't be made out to be the bad guy
I can take no more so I openly defy!
mama always said if you ain't got nothing good to say don't say it at all
now I understand why you would wait 45 minutes
until you would finally answer my face to face call
your wife?
I know she feels it too
this becomes another reason why I've chosen to do what I'm about to do
I must step away from the situation that has become untrue
though it makes me feel purple and blue
I leave cause you constantly bruise
I don't heal quickly as I use to

I'm only hurting myself when I see you

What should I do? Let me take a guess

they say, people only treat you the way you let them

you use to treat me with respect

almost as if I were your son

now a days

you keep me on the run

dodging your criticisms and now flat out abusive tongue

you've shot me down so many times as if you were firing from a gun!

the premise for our relationship was to be educational and fun

that which you have stripped me of

from day one till this day, I only tried to show and give you love

in these 17 years, you've been a part of every transitional move

I have come to you

many times asking for wisdom from the spirit of the elders

hoping the councilmen will share aged old clues

no more Mr. Nice Guy

when I walk through the threshold

it literally takes you an hour to look me in the eyes and

Say Something!

you make comments about the radio box and the voices that sing

how distasteful this song is a Sting and

the Police would bring in I am a message in the bottle

you've been coming at me most recently wanting to shatter in full throttle

I've tried to be the best model as a friend

I choose to be color blind cause it's time to bring something's to an end

I don't pretend to know everything nor do I care to

my focus has always been to do what you hired me to do

how disappointed you must be in me

mama always said be careful of what you do and be mindful of what you say

my favorite moments with you were each and every day!

whenever you would call to cancel late

I never asked you to pay

you once told me "It's not worth anything if you just give it away"

to you, I would consider it a giving spree

that's how much you meant to me

but now?

no more following and waiting to see

what the next moment of disrespect will be

I too must become

No More Mr. Nice Guy!

Peace Love Wisdom

Was I Wrong?

Chicago 2007

was I wrong for asking him to leave?
did I over look the obvious knowing he just wanted to sleep?
on the cold damp ground is where he laid his head
I gave him some money so he could go to a shelter and maybe sleep in a bed
I said, "This cannot be your American dream"
"times are hard but aren't always what they seem"
I said, "you deserve more than the feel of damp concrete on your back"
I apologized for being the one to wake him up from his no doubt peaceful nap
I stood in the pouring rain talking to him and
sharing words of encouragement hoping this might get him back on track
was I wrong for telling him he had to go?
I'm torn between what seemed to be the right thing
in hindsight, maybe I should have let him stay
until the neighbors heard a voice ring
from someone who got spooked out their wits
if the policemen came, they would have taken him for a not so favorable trip and
again I say
he deserved better
my friend asked me why didn't I invite him up to stay with me
at least for the night?
honestly, I almost did but it just didn't feel right and
the last thing I wanted was an indefinite room mate
I already had one of those who ended staying for 256 days of sunlight
Someone who has lost his insight and might to fight
have I failed in my understanding of the dharma?
could this be fate as we've come to know as karma?
he crossed the border against the governments order
now I'm faced with a dilemma
I want to help but he also has to try to help himself
so again I ask
was I wrong for asking him to leave?

peace wisdom love

Pão de Açúcar (Sugarloaf Mountain)

Chicago 2004

Listen to the Carioca's sing
hearing the sound of Samba in your ear as the church bells ring
smiling as the Carioca says "Valeo!"
each time I heard the word I swear my hair would grow!
as the arms of Cristo Redentor stretch to levitate Corcovado
oh, I just don't know
why the full moon always would glow
casting its dimmer set lights on the favela's
cloaking poverty of my bredren
there continues to show from below
they come from the north and south
such a beautiful dialect
some from the Amazon while others traveling from Bahia
quando você fala Português
it becomes much clearer
times are hard no matter where you are
first and second class citizens are as apparent as the sound of Bossa Nova
from Paulo and Jorge Santana's guitar
some home grown carioca's have yet to ride the cable cars at Pão de Açúcar
this particular day I was feeling so tranquil
I thought I would meditate
now this is where I made my first mistake
known to most as a Jamaican mystique
something so personal, yet I let them into my world to take a peek
this was the most expensive joint I ever bought!
because I was with my girl

merda! Ain't this some shit!
that's when we (I) got caught
la Policía came down on us as quick as the camera shutter would flash
they said they'd let me go if we gave them $2000 in cash
he said if I didn't pay, the Brazilian Government would deport my ass!
we came up with $900 on the spot
you gotta understand
it was our first night in Rio together so
we thought we we'd go and shop
an easy target indeed
I put my woman through that moment for some motherfucking weed

not the meditation I was hoping for
lucky for us their greed for that amount outweighed
the fact that they could have gotten more
when I think back

yeah, just leave the past in the past
another lesson learned about people in dire straights
every brother ain't a brother so don't be quick to reach for the bait
just wait
another benefit to those who meditate
no need for additional substances
patience
esperar!
let's fall back into a rhythm and begin to create
back to Pria is where I need to go
start the journey to Leme and take it slow
listen to the waves as they come crashing into the shore
this becomes the key that unlocks the transparent door
even for my woman
this is the chosen route
all the sweet things I would speak of in respect to Brazil
she sees what I've been talking about
as I sit here writing, she's out preparing for the Chicago Marathon
Help
no thank you!
this is much more than a disco tech
you can get so much more than just a dance
and that you can certainly bet
on hooking up with some sexy Brazilian girls
amazing what they could do with their looks alone on this side of the world
grande beijos para você!
to summon the powers from the mountain and from the oceans
that leads to the open seas
Gods breath is sometimes described as a northwestern breeze
kind of feels like someone licking you on your nipples just wanting to tease
our theme song from then on became "The Girl From Ipanema" by Jobim
who could have dreamed that the sun would be so bright and
the pão de açúcar would have tasted so good that night
may we forever stay in flight!
Rio de Janeiro became another birthing place
pão de açúcar became symbolic to the highs and lows of life and
on my lips
would it forever leave a taste
wisdom peace love

What's Yours? pt.I

Chicago May 2007

every man has a story
the question is will it ever be told?
some are tales of heroism while
others will leave you feeling uneasy and cold
some die as a martyr
while others will barter
giving their lives so that another might try to charter
a flight south of the border of Mexico!
didn't you know?
most tourist don't realize while chasing that worm to the bottom of the bottle
the natives don't eat that
it would be wise to sit back and relax
here is where the story gets a bit fuzzy so
you decide what's truth and what's facts!
woke up with a tranny and he was fat
back in the day we use to say
if you can't hang drink tang
at least you'd wake up with some poontane
a mouth is a mouth was the logic bouncing around in homie's brain
here comes another tale that drove a man insane
they say that first hit of crack is absolutely unlike any other
the soul becomes slave to the pipe that makes one steal from his own mother
who knew a drug could change the color of your soul?
to a pale tent that looks like it reeks the stench of death
self destruction or political corruption?
either way, it's such an empty way to die

the wells have dried up some years ago when
you basically told the world goodbye
there you stay lost in your sorrow
there's no one you can secretly borrow
for your next hit
no hit has yet to match your first
what will it take to satiate your thirst?
so came the rains to drown your heart that's been hurt cause
you don't recognize your self worth

talk is like thunder

loud and harmless
actions that might follow could make you feel lucky or charmless
good luck is received based on your karma
sometimes that crackling sound is an alarm
a tornado is creeping up behind to destroy everything in its path!
named Tornado Alley for a reason
now you do the math!
it was your choice to reside in a land where the twisters reign
it's raining cows, cars and cribs caught up in a wind tunnel's ultimate exchange
some of these tornadoes are small but reap massive havoc
how can you out guess 200 mile an hour winds if you panic?
depression sets in now the tornado resides within
the sound of thunder came again
the lightening strike was meant for a banger up the street but
in some innocent child's heart it's lodged in deep
there she sat with her sitter and two little friends
who would believe this could happen to the same family that
just buried their 21 year old son who died in Iraq while trying to defend?
America the beautiful!
that depends on which side of town you living on
though beauty is in the eye of the beholder
some stories from abroad have made others turn a cold shoulder
claiming our devil dogs are financed by rich white capitalist getting even bolder
who want's to rule the world?
stories in South Africa of tribal genocide and
deflowering innocent women and girls
to shame them so the men from her clan will not want her
the gorillas are coming to rape and murder
when will this beautiful creature purr?
again and again the assaults continue to reap havoc on a continent
if the stories are true
God, why hasn't Jesus been sent?
to eradicate the hunger, poverty and disease imposed by a crooked government
who will dare to care for the blackberries while they ripen?
only wanting the most basic entitlement of
food, clothes and shelter!
instead they must play the deadly game of "Helter Skelter"
who felt her pain while she was being circumcised?
who felt the barbaric act of cutting off her breast
so this mother couldn't feed her baby while it cries?

a country dying from hunger and disease
AIDS has devastated this land and brought a people to their knees

a lot of people who are not of color, hate seeing the others
with their palms stretched out asking, begging or pleading!
please!
now a days, you just don't know who to believe!
too many wanting to deceive
hoping they'll receive their payment for ill or supposed good deeds
somebody need to help that girl
to death she gone bleed
blood bank has the plasma but
her name ain't on the list to receive
even at the hospital they say
it's not blood but insurance you need
free clinic wasn't free when you stepped in for a minute
bomber stood in the middle of the room as you walked up in it
spin it around fool!
real cool
act like you didn't see shit! cause
he also came equipped with a glock
just as you reached for the door, you heard a pop!
everybody dropped! but
it was you who got shot
damn! Where are the cops when you need them?
they ain't never around!
homie jamming to some Pac while driving around town
cops pull him over
you won't believe what else they found
out of town warrants can catch up with you!
as soon as the cop approach the vehicle
homie just blew one round into the officers face
because of karma
you gone be facing an attempt to murder case
fool, they got your ass on tape
when the officer went down
he received a pistol whipping while trying to get up off the ground
the most incredible sound was to hear they found your ass!
now locked up in a compound
incarceration imposed because of the decisions one chose

not to eat again
cause she and her twin were too fat
her twin is but her reflection in the mirror and
there she will forever be trapped
her image of self ain't so good so

this pretty little face hovers over the bowl to protract
spits out every ounce of the meal to flush back
to the sea she was once followed
the one time they said she didn't purposely purge
was when she attempted to swallow
all of the Pacific!
with so many things on the menu
when ordering
you must be specific
If a man comes to a flight school only wanting to learn how to fly
taking off and landing aren't so important
you'd think someone would stop and wonder why?
instead approximately 4000 would die!
look at the jet liners streak through the sky
coming in at low a altitude
the suicide bombers have upgraded to Muslim Kamikaze's with
absolutely nothing to lose
within this tale tells of a president who many have declared as a fool
what exactly were you expecting from someone who
maintained a C average in school
was he to compare to Lincoln?
shot dead!
Kennedy
somebody blew off the back side of his head!
Clinton got his head blown off too!
almost impeached for insisting he didn't do the nasty!
the nasty wouldn't be that nasty if
you didn't do 20 tricks in a day
not worried about the diseases you might get
cause you wear a condom don't make it safe sex!
this game you're playing is called Russian Roulette or
wherever you might be born
the total sum of your earnings go to the pimp you been running from

these stories are told by the naive, vulnerable and the dumb
by the warriors, poets and drunkards who only drink white rum
are you as adventurous as Captain Jack Sparrow or
is your mind narrow?
does it run through your veins freezing the bones marrow?
all aboard the Black Pearl!
to sail the Egyptian Sea's searching for Pharaohs and
God's servants who wrote the scriptures in the bible
could the pilot not hit the ejection button as the fighter plane spiraled?

out of control!
is how some of the youth are described in American culture
not having a sense of direction nor
the desire to excel in something positive to its absolute perfection
for some
it's faulted because of their complexion
so many young men of color
are dying in succession or
in a precinct line up, they say you fit the description
of the bank robbers who played doctor and issued out prescriptions
for life, one is imprisoned
the death penalty is the sentence the others got
cause they're the ones who were killers of cops
another story gone bad cause some refuse to stop and
smell the roses
hurry before the door of opportunity closes
to leave to fate
a story that is heart wrenching or immeasurably great
again the question is asked
out of all the stories to be told
when we meet to greet
will you be warm or cold?
will you show hate and
wanna debate the style of my clothes? or
will you be the one
who just comes blazing through my door?
What's yours?
Peace Love Wisdom

☞ Wake Up My Brothers!

01.25.09 (rest stop on the Ohio Turnpike)

who was the shooter?

the soul looter?

street polluter?

leaving this debris behind

bodies falling down while throwing up them gang signs

another unsolved crime

is this the true sign of the times?

who you represent?

shorty had a dream about becoming the second black president

till some fool came by needing to vent

God, why hasn't Jesus been sent?

I said Jesus not Jesus

Jesus wore sandals while Jesus wore them timberland boots

Christ wore a robe while brothers pants are at his knees nice and loose and

Timber!

another body falls to the ground

America's Most Wanted says he always makes a funny sound

just before somebody gets popped!

John Walsh said if you hear somebody cry out nigga

you better drop! but

stop! that's the typical call on the block

like somebody crying out wolf around the clock 24/7!

they say heaven can wait

it's also said that it's never too late

to escape but

who can outrun a bullet?

oh yea! maybe Superman but

what if it were his evil twin who threw it?

thrown off a high horse and it dried up all his spinal fluid!

paralyzed cause some homie shot him from behind

shot in the back by another brother with no spine!

it's hard enough trying to stay out of the welfare line

trying to stay off the block selling them nickels and dimes

who is the shooter that took the shimmer from his shine?

we need to intervene before he commits the next crime

I fear it could be my daughter next

then I'll be behind bars with a life sentence

insisting the killers ass whopping was heaven sent!
500 murdered children on these Chicago streets just don't make sense!
in the time frame of one year
another falls to the ground as fast as a grieving mothers tears
who was the shooter?
the soul looter?
street polluter?
leaving debris behind
bodies removed but there lay another dried up bloodline
another child dead on the streets for his mama to find
who's willing to throw out a lifeline?
I sign my name on the dotted line
reach out for one and
watch him run
to you instead of the lure of the gun!
It feels like we're living on the Gaza Stripe
how did our youth get so fully fucking equipped?
launching out the word nigga like it was a grenade
I have a picture of two young brothers spray painting KKK
as part of their gang symbol
Willie Lynch would be so proud to know he still resides in your mental
my brothers wake the fuck up! cause
this is becoming detrimental!
Global Warming is also being created by
your ancestors at the bottom of the sea!
this was the cost for them wanting to be free
they as slaves were bound by chains
you are free yet bound to a gang
run by the CEO's that would bring
$into your hood guns, crack and cocaine
$pimping your punk ass for chump change
cause he knows you're a hustler
won't take no shit from them punk bitch busters!
especially those who call themselves the law
perfect for them cause here's your next flaw
you the only one the camera saw
in a courthouse that remembers your father

I guess it's true what they say
like father like son, you too didn't even bother to step away
here's the family reunion as a child you would pray for
now you got a life time to catch up once they lock them prison doors!
I ask

who is the shooter?

the soul looter?

street polluter

leaving debris behind

bodies removed but there lay another dried up bloodline

what ever happened to the peace sign?

with so much to live for

now it's wasted time!

this becomes the saddest of all your crimes

wanting to rule more than self

you never stopped to actually find you!

your Morpheus side that says

take the red pill instead of the blue!

wake up my brothers, wake up! ➥

➥ peace love wisdom ➥

Wicked Ways

October 4th 2006 Chicago

Straight from the News:

here I was
wet behind my baby ears
I say I was just a little boy
mama's girlfriend used me as a freaky little sex toy
I can't imagine back then how she found so much joy
she was an absolute pedophile
she tried to take away one of my most precious gifts
she tried to take away my smile
while
all along it was her in absolute denial
Now
turn on the news and hear about this shit every day
even government officials taking time out to play
how about the little girl who was held captive for over eleven years
kept locked up in a basement for so long
as the water filled the room about six feet high
nobody knew these were her tears of fear
she finally got away cause he accidently left his car keys on the window pane
she didn't know how to drive but sped away in the pouring rain
cause she ran away her abductor became distraught and
how symbolic as the roles reversed
he threw himself in front of a run away train!
that moment of impact still could not measure up to her shame and pain
years of therapy will be needed before this soul will be able to regain

they call it Amber Alert cause
he's turned on by her knee high stockings and the green plaid skirt
so he flirts!
she screams out "mama, mama make him go way!"
he throws her into the trunk of his car in the middle of the day
flyers passed out around the country asking "Have you seen my baby today?"
will she too find a way to escape? or
is this another tragic tale of a pedophile and his wicked ways?

preacher, preacher
help me talk to God

he said come to confession then confesses it's the child's soul he wants to rob

there he stands wearing the holy robe while offering communion

50 little boys victimized and sodomized now

afraid to go to the priests holy reunion

mama and papa have no idea that little Bobby now knows how to give head

thinking the only thing going on in bible study are the holy scriptures being read instead

Bobby comes home with cum stains on the side of his mouth

mommy tucks him in at bed time

little Bobby screams out "Ouch!"

"mommy, my soul hurts" now

he'll spend a lifetime cleansing his soul from the priest's dirt!

it becomes another tragic tale of a pedophile and his wicked ways

teacher, teacher

I just don't understand

this trigonometry is difficult, could you give me a hand?

"yes" she said

cause you're a good student, I'm willing to take a chance

now open up your book and pull down your pants

first she gave him a hand job then sucked off his "triga"

they did the "nometry dance"

she told him if he kept his studying hard like that!

his grades would certainly advance

for the rest of the year she would become the tutor oh yeah

from the "roota to the toota"

who'da thought she was setting him up

to commit a crime based on placebo love

gave him a pistol and said "don't forget to wear the gloves"

she said "if you kill my husband, I'll forever be your girlfriend"

here is where another tragic tale begins of

a pedophile and her wicked ways

zoo keeper, zoo keeper

where is your home?

he said "I like to sleep in the wild where the buffalo roam"

all the four legged creatures are afraid to fall asleep

they tell tales of an upright polar bear who does a late night creep

they say it's imperative to take turns while grazing on the grass

he likes to sneak up on you then plug you in the ass

let's just leave that one alone cause this shit is just wrong here we go again just another freaky day

reasons for mans scandalous behavior makes no sense no matter what they say

it just becomes another tragic tale of a freak or a pedophile and his wicked ways

Mad Cow Disease

motherfucker please!

what about AIDS? somebody went to Africa and fucked a monkey for days

these polar bears have been passing these diseases around

ever since he built his ships then insisted he found

the "New World"!

back to that government official who was suppose to be voting cause

we know how important it is to vote?

anyway, he was voting

hoping a bill would finally pass instead

there he was in his own little world

text messaging an underage boy, hoping he'd get to tag that ass

blamed it on alcohol and said he'll put himself in rehab

he was actually appointed to his office to help protect children

from predators in full throttle

who did the background check on this public official

who was suppose to be a role model for

our troops who are fighting against those who think

American's ain't nothing but pussy's, punks and fags

absolutely no disrespect to the gay community but

by putting himself in rehab for alcohol

it's like seeking diplomatic immunity

when in fact

it just becomes another tragic tale of a pedophile and his wicked ways

Mr. Marines

it's time to pack up your bags

on the other side of the world offending the American flag now

stripped of duties and your special force dog tags

look at you and your homies about to get court marshaled

went to fight for a cause but only wanting to give partial

these soldiers had a completely different agenda

said they wanted to be all they could be but were nothing but pretenders

turned out to be nothing but sex offenders

took turns raping that little Iraqi girl

I guess they wanted to know what it was like getting some cuchie

from a baby on the other side of the world

twirled her around and they she lay buried six feet underground

with the rest of her family who received round after round after round of

bullets from our freedom fighters, peace makers

from our pedophiles and their wicked ways

Dear Papa
I' m so confused and down right sad
I don't understand how you are my biological father yet
you are also my baby's dad
dear papa
I just don't understand how this can be
how you are also my little sisters baby's daddy?
I guess we are all from the same family tree
is it true that mama is my eldest sister?
people say she too is your daughter
papa, papa
why are you holding our baby under water?
he can't swim!
you said if he's not telling a lie then God will let him drown
if he is then god will make him stick around so
you can punish him with your big black dick every time he frowns
lucky for him he wasn't telling a lie
you put that black stick in my mouth every time I cry!
dear papa
I haven't seen mama for weeks
there's a stench coming from the basement that
keeps me awake when I try to fall asleep
what are those funny looking boxes in the other room?
stop!
put me down papa!
please daddy!
I'm carrying another one of your babies in my womb!
those funny looking boxes were actually caskets and
now one becomes her tomb
here becomes another tragic tale for an innocent soul with
another pedophile and his wicked ways!
if you know of a child that is in an abusive home
don't sit there looking stupid
motherfucker pick up the phone!
if you don't, you too are that pedophile
if you see someone lurking around the corners
call the police cause somebody might become guest at the
county morgue being dissected by the coroner
please take a stand and help out your fellow man
especially the children

peace love wisdom

Welcome to the Ghetto

born as a chi town ghetto child
things back in the day sho nuf' got buck wild
all my time as a shorty spent on the south to west side
brothers out on the street corners hustling from day to day
everybody hoping for a better way
cost of living soaring to the sky
kids toting guns around hoping to die
everywhere you turn
you can hear another mother's cry
feel the pain and sorrow as she cries cause
she also died deep inside
this child was who she was living for
to know they'll never again come running through that door
how do you start all over?
there's no such thing as a four leaf clover
welcome to the ghetto
shattered dreams fills the air while the past many just forgot
broken glass filled the play lots
from broken 40's and vials once filled with rocks
the cops are nowhere to be found when we heard gunshots
playing "cowboy and Indians" seemed to be a game of pretend but
wound up being early training in recognizing how to defend
fight for our rights with persistence
join forces and make this one hell of a revolution
to fight against any injustice
we will stand firm but not be rambunctious

not who we are
every time you called him a nigga
that's another brother who didn't get too far
call him Doctor, Professor or maybe even Astronaut not
bitches and twitches who at one timed or another copped
cops roll through and y'all get caught
another brother to send into the system
in general population he now has to walk
through these streets painted like hallways and cell blocks of
this over populated ghetto

he gone get caught for sure
he might get passed around as the cell block whore
got caught up again
now something creeping within his skin
let him out in five
that fool barely made it out alive
goes back to the hood and tells tales of how he survived
he's a hero in the hood now so
all the chicken heads let him in between their thighs
girl number 7 gave birth to his baby yesterday
don't nobody know he also gave her AIDS
doctor said the baby's infected too
there she sits in the county with nobody to call nor
does she have a clue
she's only 15 so how is she suppose to know what to do?
what would you do if this was you?
little homie knows that shorty is his
he said it's her fault she got pregnant
shit!
it is what it is!
he said he don't care about none of his kids
his daddy wasn't around to fill that gap in his life
so he looks into the distance with that blank look in his eyes
then simply asks, why?
sun sets on the ghetto tonight
without fail, some more fools break into another gun fight
the innocent ones must duck and hide
children lying in bed in absolute fright
ghetto living seems to be the same no matter where you go
from the east side of Cali to the North Pole in Chicago
from the rough streets of NYC to the favela's in Rio de Janeiro
shit
welcome to the ghetto!

Wisdom Love Peace

Bob Said...(the eleventh hour)

Chicago January 2011

★ Bob tell them ★
get up, stand up
stand up for your rights
him say get up, stand up
don't give up the fight!
the light shines bright
though this conscious dred has gone into flight
sight enhanced as his voice would dance
in the mind of a man who wanted to advance
into realms of consciousness
how blessed I am to digest these messages of wisdom
Bob say, "Soon Come"
morse codes being translated on the drum
calculating the sum of righteousness from
Jamaica to Belgium, from Canada to England
from Chicago to Scotland
from the heavens to hell where the fiery rivers run!
Bob say "upon a rock I rest my head..."
to the rivers I go to wash my dreds
visions of prisons as seas of oppression still run through the continent
I and I long for the messengers sent
Jesus bless us with your divinity
Great Buddha calm and sooth us with your meditation of serenity
Allah watches over all of humanity!
could it be like Haile Sallasie, Bob was reincarnated energy?
representing Jah Rastafari as his Almighty!
calling out in such sweet melody
calling out for an "Uprising"
teach the youth to stop this genocide them bring!
how many more must be left behind to cry?
how many more must be left to die?
Bob said "No Woman No Cry" he also say
no man is an island so "Why Should I bend down my head and cry"? why?
though "I'm Hurting Inside"
I must get up stand up, stand up for my right!
I say get up stand up, don't give up the fight!
Bob him ask, "Is This Love?"
this is the same question I ask the young bloods

while them spilling each others precious black oil
turmoil follows around every block!
there he stands with his hat cocked
Bob say, "Who the cap fit let him wear it"
within this beautiful black body somebody unloads a full clip!
at the funeral, mama cries out "Johnny Was A Good Man" and
with "So Much Trouble" in the world
who would want to bite the hand that
wants to help you to become a real man
that gave such "Positive Vibrations"
within this "Rat Race" I and I need to develop patience and

we should be "Forever Loving Jah"
as I look to the northern star, I'm "Giving Thanks and Praises" cause
I know you wrote the law!
"Three Little Birds" pitch by my window and there I saw
me, me, me!
running and "Running Away"
away from "Babylon System"
GD's, Vice Lords, Cobra's, Latin Kings and all I didn't mention
my young brothers, I hope you stop and take a listen cause
there's a "Natural Mystic" blowing in the air!
put down your guns young soldiers cause we need you to care!
this "Concrete Jungle" is man made
by hundreds of thousands that are dropped off in unmarked graves
by the "Slave Drivers" who still have you in their strong grip
that has you standing on the edge of a mother fucking cliff!
"Soul Captive"
so you slip deep into the pit
left behind never to join in this "Exodus" Movement of Jah people
Bob said, "Get up stand up
stand up for your rights
him say, get up stand up
don't give up the fight!
Feeling like a "Crazy Ballhead" cause you locked up in them penitentiary
judge says you'll serve at least a century before your chances for parole
there you stand alone in this "Rainbow Country" you call home
when Bob crooned out "Baby, baby we Got a date.
Oh baby don't you be late…"
he wasn't referring to your cell mate
9:00pm lights out and again your ass get raped and can't escape
these thugged out homosexual tendencies
Remember when you were hanging on the block with your pants

dropped down passed your knees
walking around looking like you were in shackles
baffled why the law keeps you on high profile
your look is only sexy to the same sex pedophiles
meanwhile, you go and gun down another "Buffalo Soldier"
he was going to school to be a lawyer
had a dream about being a legitimate employer of misfits just like you
now who will "Wait In Vain" while the ripples flow through
from the heathens who kill simply because the hat was red instead of blue
just when we were about to celebrate the "Black Mans Redemption"
another youth became attached to a sentence
he probably couldn't even read cause
in school he never paid attention
like the "Stiff Necked Fool" him don't know that
his wealth is in his righteousness!
with this wrong interpretation, they don't see how blessed they really are
instead of an actual joy ride

"Mr. Brown" and his homies get into a stolen car to do multiple drive byes!
Mommie says "miho, miho get up!" and in her arms there he dies!
just another passerby!
15th on this block who lost his life
Mommy says again "Miho, miho vamos!" "Get up miho!"
"get up and stand up
stand up for your life!"
she said "get up stand up
baby, please don't look into the light
get up stand up
please don't give up the fight!

Fo Flights flame came from the many of nights
while meditating with Bob under candle light
wisdom from Marley gave more insight like
"Guava Jelly", I taste the bitter sweetness of truth
as it would shin so bright within my soul
no more "Guiltiness" or acting out of control cause
come "High Tide or low Tide" I'm gone be your friend! so
when you're "Coming in from the Cold" it's easier to blend in
shed that man made name that references the blackness of your skin
Bob say in every mans chest there beats a heart
I raise the rod of Moses that possess the spirit of God
it's time to part the oceans
a true "Soul Rebel" sharing real love and emotion

it's time to put aside our differences and show some more devotion
Bob say, "Judge Not" so stop the gun shots!
we could have the biggest party on the block
reconnecting what has been lost since
the beginning of this self imposed Holocaust
the real battle has yet to be fought

Bob said "Get Up, Stand Up
stand up for you rights

him say get up stand up
don't give up the fight!
Bob say
get up stand up
stand up for your rights!

Wisdom

Last Hit

December 19th 2006

I'm about to open up my mind
light up a fat one and just unwind
spend a little more time
enhancing these skills to rhyme
I take another puff
then slowly exhale
it happens every time without fail
the words start pouring out of me
like a hail storm
so I might spit into the mic!
the words will either cause a disturbance or
insight some joy and delight
full is how I'm starting to feel
as I take another hit of the fat girl
stuffed with either some good old Sensimilla or
toke on that Hawaiian and it'll make you choke
from some words so honest and sincere
Amazing the people who have sat through some of these pages and
with me they would shed a tear
not for me but
for the streams felt for years of
feelings locked within their own souls
I remember this brother on a flight to NY lost control
he cried for half the flight
told me about how his father subconsciously prepped him
with memorable moments before they experienced that unforgettable night
now the smell blends in
a stimulating mix of lavender and nag champa incense
used as the ancients did so long ago
smoking from the peace pipe opened up the world of the shadows
the spirit world!
here's where the mind expands and grows
my bloodline on my papa's side comes from African and Seminole
my mama said her grand mother was a half breed
mixed with French and Native American
from what tribe? she said The Navaho!
I can only imagine how beautiful she was
many nights I think I speak to her when I'm buzzed

while I write these words
I speak from the heart and only want to share love
Streams of Consciousness are more than random words slurred
listen to that piece called "To Be"
hear the essence and power of a simple verb
you can either dance across the clouds
swim the oceans from Alaska to motherfucking Laos
one more hit and I might pass out!
that's when I heard a voice inside me scream out and shout
this is your ascension into the next dimension!
while you write these words, never forget to mention
that life is only what you make it!

if you feel someone trying to hold you back
you gotta stand up strong and shake it!
take yourself to another level
just cause shit don't always go your way
don't always mean you can't win the gold medal
and the streams continue to flow
winding down another good year in the city of Chicago
we about to get hit with a blizzard of snow!
Cu Cu called and said they got hit in Colorado
I serenade this moment cause it's that time of year
there have been so many reasons to shed so many tears
from the loss of my father and cousin Danny and
not to mention, my girl thought she should disappear
from my life these positive spirits have gone
as I take this last drag
it's time to stand up proud and strong
my system will continue to flow out poems and songs
the flight of the Falcon is about to commence
for me
the herbs did help to weave through these delicate moments and make sense
I have found my way in and out of some of the most incredible moments
there's no way you could consider this to be a mere coincidence
there are spirits guiding us to our next moment of existence so
thank you for my next lesson
each time I meditate with you, I'm never second guessing
I know I must be honest with myself
if I continue to puff from you, fat girl
you will begin to disrupt my world and health
that would make it
you, a negative

instead of opening the doors
you'd knock me out like a sedative!
one more hit and we're through
I need to get back to the other things that I do
if I ever need you again, I'll definitely let you know but
for now, I need to go solo cause
I'm about to open up my mind and
let the streams continue to flow!
marry jane reefer bud spliff joint
weed chronic smoke hocus pocus
marijuana chalice ganga smokey smoke
white russian kush fat girl dr wu flame boa
dro northern lights
buddha peace wisdom!

Wounded Lion

Chicago June 28th 2007

I'm a wounded lion in the jungle
instead of a mighty roar
I've been reduced to mumble
with that breath I lick my scars
Lord knows I've battled with fire in my eyes and fought hard
who knew they would come with weapons of mass destruction
poisonous darts and instruments designed for blood suction
as I lay here masked by the heavy shrubs
I must continue moving cause I've left a trail of blood
I can hear them coming in the distance as they carry in their hearts
hate and wickedness never knowing peace and love
the darts they've fired have pierced my skin
there was some type of fire used cause I can feel it kicking in
it burns my flesh while singeing my soul
the hyena's are out in large numbers and on patrol
might I sleep for a while or play dead if they approach and
begin poking me with poles
slowly I rise still disguised by the bush
these blood thirsty savages won't stop this relentless push
I am king of the jungle!
as I scan into the distance
I take a moment to reflect and feel humble
as a zebra runs by me, he glances back and tries to warn
"they're coming, they're coming, run!"
bang!
was the next sound heard from those steel dart guns

he no longer fears me because they're coming for both our hides
now the adrenaline's kicking in
fight or flight is my plight!
I feel no pain and I seemed to have made a friend
If we survive
I shall hunt you no more
the zebra's strips changed and blossomed
into wings and carried us through a secret door
that led us into a hidden cave
for miles we journeyed before coming to a rest
what a sight to see, a zebra and lion flying through the trees

this zebra is actually wanting to save me, the king of the jungle!?!
what could happen next?
a sacrifice was now offered to save my life
the zebra offered his flesh and blood so that I might regain strength to fight
this was an offer this carnivore could not except
you've saved my life once already
so forever I am in your debt

to you I vow!
as king of the jungle I bow to you, zebra
as the pale full moon rises in the night sky it begins the season of the Libra
"puncture my flesh with those razor sharp teeth then with those
vise grip jaws a little at a time to begin your needed feed" said the zebra
like a cub sucking from its mothers nipple
I the lion quenched my hunger as the blood would ripple
through the hip of this sacrificial lamb
"When I meet those two legged creatures again
they will come to know who I am"
just enough blood was taken so that this zebra could survive
amazing outside the caves entrance formed a line
there stands hundreds more wanting to nurse me back to health
after drinking blood for ten days
I the lion was beginning to feel like myself
some animals were brought in who were also struck
by these killing metal darts
"who knows the evil that lurks in their heart" said the panther
as he took his last breath
he like all the others would ask that I consume their flesh
so that I might nourish myself back to be the true king
"avenge us, your loyal servants for
you wear the mane for a purpose"
the monkey's came in to sharpen my claws
three female lions appeared so that I might
remove this stagnant energy from my balls
for me they would bare six male cubs each
I the lion am starting to feel truly like the king again and I begin to teach
my new born how to respect the land
trust in your kingdom but never trust in that creature they call man
the roar of the beast has returned and vibrates throughout the plains
I am no longer the wounded beast who's blood rains
the hyena's run in fear sensing things are about to change
I am coming for their hides with a new and healthy pride
as for man

you are not exempt from my food chain
that bullet is still lodged in my shoulder blade and
it fires off thoughts of revenge constantly in my brain
I am King
I will forever reign
King of the Jungle!
Wisdom Respect!

What's Yours pt.2

Chicago June 2007

want some
get some
bad enough
take some
stuck his hand in the cookie jar
now he on the run
from the law!
who saw him on video
playing stick up kid
went into the bank
shit went mad wrong now
look what you done gone and did
you told the teller he was moving too slow
shot the security guard as he reached for the door
damn teller wanted to tell!
don't be no hero cause this job don't pay that well
he reached for the alarm
now he laid on the floor bleeding in his co-workers arms
the gunman wanted his transaction in non sequential numbers
ordered everyone on the floor cause he would cap every runner!
now he's on the run with tweedle dee, tweedle dumb and dumber
one of these fools left behind a piece of paper
with an address and a number
one of these cats works as a part time plumber
pimped out driving a Hummer
something just don't fit
now it's time to get caught!
three weeks on the Vegas Strip
it was your girl who gave the Police their tip
she was willing to stay quiet and just spend the money
you pissed her off when she read that text message from your secret honey
never push a woman in that direction
video taped again except now you're making a confession
tricking on your boys who you swore you'd never tell on

Dee and dumb still on the run but
not for long cause the law has built up a case against y'all and it's strong!
neither one has a passport so they must hide and try to slide

under radar they managed to stay for a while
greed kicked in so their guns once again went POW!
cross country chase with the FBI Profilers
figuring out how and where the next target would be
on America's Most Wanted so the whole country will see
your MO ain't secret no more!
Bin Laden gone have to wait before we come knocking on his door!
rolled up on a roadblock
greeted by 50 cops!
with pistols and shotguns aiming at the center of your lids
y'all wanna do a Butch Cassidy and Sundance Kid
romancing this idea of death
one says to the other
"I'll meet you at the crib!"
with the pedal pushed to the metal
they tried to break through the barricades
tires were flattened cause the spikes were laid!
every cop sprayed bullets that found their target
now the stolen car becomes a grave
souls lost in this destructive path
slipping into darkness glorifying that bullet bath!
there they lay with their brains splattered on the dash!
who did the math?
200 bullets from the law on a cross country war path
I say live by the gun
die by the gun
let's flip to another script
see who else is on the run!

wisdom peace

Bad Idea

Chicago June 2007

you're an enemy in me casa!
step pass the threshold bet your bottom dollar you gone holla!
something's about to sting your dome
that's what you get coming in unannounced inside my home
walked in thinking you were a pimp
hobbled away deflated with a limp
once I'm through with you
everyone shall refer to you as the neighborhood gimp!

who tried to take advantage of someone in their sleep
I lay with one eye opened so I heard you trying to creep
my crib is booby trapped with devices that will knock you off your feet
you stepped into the wrong domain cause I got some techniques!
they say "He who feels it, knows it" well
tonight I'm feeling like a poet!
I'm gonna whisper in your ear a sonnet
the words shall vibrate causing chronic
pain to the brain
as you come to know my reality
you shall also come to know my name
over the ledge of the deck you go bracing for more pain!
you have entered into the house of a crazed and insane man
you'd better call the police if you can! cause
I'm about to dance on your face
break your femur in several place
is this the moment you hoped you were in a dream?

this might not have been thought out so well
once I'm finally through with you
I'll call the cops so they can haul your ass off to jail
but for now?
huh
Bad Idea! boom! bang! pow!

Peace Wisdom

I Don't Mean To Be Rude...

Chicago March 2009

Welcome to the Fo Flight Poetry Night
There's only one rule while we're sharing some insight
PLEASE
Respect the mic!
excuse me sir
might I have a word with you?
hum
I don't mean to be rude but
you fucking up the mood
I'm trying to spit some consciousness into the mic but
you're just giving me the blues
I don't mean to be rude but
you ain't part of this groove so
shut the fuck up man cause

you about to be removed!
I like to think I'm just as strong as the next but
when it comes to my poetry
I'm sensitive about my shit
vexed on why you keep talking over the mic
why you scream across the room with all your might
like
"hey Bobby, get me a drink"
I hope he brings back a cup of water and
a life jacket cause you bout to sink
deep into this lyrical mind
you the special dedication to this here rhyme
why is it always them wine heads first to step out of line?
hear the chime as it gets ready to vibrate inside your dome
maybe you should have kept your ass at home alone and
whacked off your little pixie stick
you know
the one you keep stroking wile acting like a motherfucking prick
I've stood at the mic in a room loaded with gang bangers and
received more respect than this!
the theme for the night was to kick back and chill
instead you came ill and spilled your disrespect
I'm gone stand strong on the mic and absolutely with no regrets!
I've seen twitches like you before
who don't know the meaning of respect so
I'd suggest you go back to school and
pick up a text book

look up Buddha and recognize the inner journey that he took
this is the hook
this is the hook to sit in silence and stillness
why you wanna come and try to kill this?
your illness becomes moments of guiltiness you possess
without ever wanting to bless some consciousness!
look
I don't mean to rude but
you fucking up the mood!
I'm trying to spit consciousness into the mic yet
you keep giving me your blues
I don't mean to rude but
you ain't part of my groove so
so shut the fuck up man cause
yousa' bout to be removed!

there she go feeling all booshie

think everybody in the room wanna hit that cuchie

put a lil, lil liquor in her now she's acting loopy

snoopy wouldn't hit that slit

once he saw you acting like a bitch!

disrespecting the mic and

you just wouldn't quit!

acting like gardenia and sandalwood is the fragrance of your shit!

another missed opportunity for you to grow within this tree

I came to bless you and the mic but

I guess you just couldn't see

as the sweat poured down my face

I'm still gone give you all of me

cause I fight for what I believe

you had a chance to come and swim within these seas

instead you stay locked up in the pathetic world that you call yourself

didn't want to give respect to this band of poets and their incredible wealth

well you snooze and you lose

shut the fuck up girl cause you about to be removed!

let you go out and talk to the asphalt pavement

ask the concrete exactly what this piece meant

I came as a messenger of God so

who do you represent?

I guess you got your money's worth

based on the girth of your mouth and all the liquor you slurped

now you feelings are about to get hurt!

turf toe is what I'm about to get

it's time for you to be removed from this poetry set!

I don't mean to be rude but

you fucking up the mood

I'm trying to spit some consciousness into the mic but

you keep giving me the blues

I don't mean to be rude but

you really gotta realize

you ain't part of this groove so

shut the fuck up man cause you bout to be removed!

jamming on a piece inspired by Robert Nesta Marley

he came in a vision one night to share these words then said

"Go rock the next party!"

from the first phrase others could hardly hear

before you and your peeps came

you must have had another taste of some barley beer

well
cheers!
I raise my glass to you and make a toast cause
it's time for your ass to disappear
the theme to the piece was "Bob Said..." get up, stand up
him say stand up for your rights
now it's time for you to get up and stand up
gather up all your shit in sight
I said get up stand up!
motherfucker have a good night! cause
you have been dismissed
read these puma's as they kiss your ass!
maybe next time we meet
you'll be more open to the bath
so rich in minerals from the spirits that some have dubbed as witchcraft
now it's time to get back into the groove
have so more fun with the respecters and
not to waste my time with motherfuckers you!
I don't mean to be rude but
you fucking up the mood
I'm trying to spit some consciousness into the mic yet
you keep giving me the blues
I don't mean to be rude but
you really ain't part of this groove so
shut the fuck up man cause
you about to be remove!
I Don't Mean to Be Rude...
Peace Wisdom

Love Your Brother

Chicago 2004

you gotta love your brother
love your sister
respect your elders cause
Jah is watching you
Jah is watching over you and
he sees everything that you do
you say your brother has done wrong
every time you see him
he's singing the same old sad song
why is the man who is truly in need
constantly overlooked and
the white collared executive turns out to be the crook
stealing clothes off the backs and food from the table
we've gotta look out for those who are not able cause
you gotta love your brother
love your sister
respect your mama and papa cause
Jah is watching you!
as we approach the beginning of a new dawn
there's a decision to make
will we turn our backs on one another? or
protect what Jah continues to create?
look in your heart then you will discover
look first with your third eye
now open your physical side eyes wide
soon you shall realize
fate of mankind is up to I and I
the only way we will survive
is if we Love, Love, Love
love your brothers
love your sisters
respect our mama's and papa's too
remember
Jah is watching over you
repeat... fade Peace

Feeling it Deep...the poet

Chicago February 2011

I'm a poet
I don't need to wear on my chest to show it cause
As soon as you hear me croon you'll know it!
While I flow it
Dredlocks dropped is where I grow it
Words whispered in the wind for me to drip through my pen
I subscribe to the Streetwise
There the peoples poetry cries and lies
In the gutters and clutters with crack vials and discarded rubbers
tricks turned out by 15 year old mothers
cause poetry comes from the soil of mother earth
from the nooks and crannies stems my next verse
I say poetry comes from the soil of mother earth
Because of her cries
Within each and every piece I recite
You can hear her hurt
I remember as a child
When Superman formed The justice Leagued
To Flash, The Seven Angels, Wonder Woman and to all the rest
He said, "For you, I kryptonite bleed! As long as you do what you do!
Just do it with your absolute best!"
Not one time did he ask his comrades to wear that S on their chest
What turned you on about me
Well, that exactly what you're always gonna see
My originality!
The totality of a mix
It would be like, huh
Superman asking Batman to remove his Cow
Next thing you hear is a "Bing, Bop, Boom!"
Then Bow!
Wow!
Like a tracking device on Batman's Mobile
Somebody's trying to steal his identity
cause poetry comes from the soil of mother earth
from the nooks and crannies stems my next verse
I say poetry comes from the soil of mother earth
Because of her cries

Within each and every piece I recite
You can hear her hurt

From that soil my poetry becomes flawless
Lawless!
I'm reaching for my dreams while you're standing 69 balls less
I guess you're not impressed
My whacked out grooves
I wear Fo Flight on my chest
Taught by a Shaolin Monk
Mad Monkey is on my mind and ready to take the test
Why you wanna come hate on me?
Say my brother can't you see?
This shit could have been done so easily
But you want me to sell out
I guess since I'm not a member
I lose my clout!
Which means, I had to buy in to be your friend
Now that makes we wanna grin!
Blacklisted by them all
While my poetry still flows like the Niagara Falls
To drench the soils again
Drench them Fo Flight
Drench Them Fo Flight!
69 Times Again!
cause poetry comes from the soil of mother earth
from the nooks and crannies stems my next verse
I say poetry comes from the soil of mother earth
Because of her cries
Within each and every piece I recite
You can hear her hurt
Spirits come and speak with me
Come and speak with we
Whisper in my ear some more of that poetry
Come flow with me
I bet you'll quickly agree
Even the butterflies come to speak
Bees buzz a sweet rap with me while letting me feed them honey
I come in peace
From the heavens and hell do these stories rain for me to tell
I am a poet...

Peace Love Wisdom

Baby Jane

01.31.09 Chicago

I was told this story late one night
the night I went deeper into the mind of Fo Flight
this story never made the late night news
buckle up cause here come a tale of 'lil baby Jane's blues!

Lil baby Jane gets raped by her uncle
told her not to tell or he'd kill her with his bare knuckles and
chuckles while swigging on some old E
He whispers in her ear "this is all you were meant to be!"
Here mama refuses to see
the bruises on baby Jane's face and
the cigarette burns on her thighs and knees
Sweet Jesus come from the sky and throw this child a bone!
Instead mama goes out tricking and leaves baby Jane home all alone
with uncle pedophile!
Behind her smile resides absolute fear cause
this shits been going on for the last 5 years
Her tear glands have completely dried up
For breakfast lunch and dinner Baby Jane gets fucked
Instead of a pacifier, it's her loving uncle she's got to suck
he said, "Lets play prison"
while every hole he tries to stuff and bust a nut
once again baby Jane's gotta to knuckle!
who gone stop the reign?
Who gone show some real love for Baby Jane?
OOoooooooooo do you? do you? do you?

cause
It's a crying shame
Her mama won't except the blame
She said her brother loves her lil baby candy cane
that why Baby Jane ain't got a friend to her name
She's so scared, so, so scared she's afraid to scream!
Is this to be her claim to fame?
Uncle pedophile is deep inside her head, he's so deep inside her brain
they say when it rains it pours! Poor little baby's about to get some more!

Cause

Friends of the family been invited in to make Baby Jane their little whore
What good will ever walk through her bedroom door?
Ain't gone be her mama now that's for sure!
OOoooooooooooo do you? do you? do you?
Do you love your Baby Jane?
Tell me mama, why won't you ease her away from this pain?
Gone put a bullet in her brain cause
Your brother ain't gone change cause
To you, he use to do the same
this is such a sad, sad song to sing!
OOOooooooooooo do you? do you? do you?
Do you love your Baby Jane?
Around the world, in a different language, this shit is all the same
Great God please take away their pain!
OOoooooooooo do you? do you? do you?
do you love your Baby Jane?
I say ooooooooo do you? do you? do you?
Do you love your Baby Jane?
They say
DCFS was responding to a call
Neighbors said it sound like somebody
keep getting slammed into the wall!
Have you ever seen Jackie Chan's "The Big Brawl"?
Baby Jane is ready to stand up and walk tall or die trying!
Mama was in the other room flying high on some crack
Uncle pedophile took a couple of hits then tried another attack
Baby Jane was hiding a hammer behind her back!
This child snapped then cracked this motherfucker up side his head!
Singing some Curtis Mayfield "Freddy's Dead" she say "Yeah that what I said!"
Everything done turned the color red
With all her might, she strokes his head in her bed but
Not the strokes he was hoping for
While screaming out "Don't touch me no more!"
Baby Jane done gone for broke!
Now he's laid out in a pool of his own blood while twitching on the floor
Po-Po finally breaks through the door and read this girl her rights
She was suppose to have the rights to life
Mama's in the other room now armed with a knife
Then sliced the veins in her wrists

Bled out and died just as Baby Jane came in and
gave her a goodbye kiss
To a mama she said she never had and

to a childhood never to be missed!

come back to the hook and spit

OOoooooooo do you? do you? do you?

Do you love your Baby Jane?

Why wouldn't you take her away from this pain?

OOoooooooo do you? do you? do you?

Do you love your Baby Jane?

Why you smoke away your brains?

Forced her to spill your pedophile brothers membranes!

Baby Jane done gone insane!

Now the State's got your Princess bound and uncrowned in chains

Mama! That's your Baby Jane!

OOoooooooooooooo do you? do you? do you?

Do you really love your Baby Jane?

This is when she needs her mama or somebody who knows her real name

Do you? do you? Do you really love your Baby Jane?

This is such a sad, sad song to sing

OOoooooooooo do you? do you? do you?

Do you love your Baby Jane?

Tell me mama, do you? do you? do you? Do you love your Baby Jane?

This is such sad, sad song to sing

Love Wisdom Peace

For My Family

Chicago 1996

for my family
I hide my love
for my family
my freedom has flown away
on the wings of a dove
for my family
I live their insecurities
for my family
I again must learn humility
for my family
I must follow the code of my peoples way
for my family
I must live their lives from day to day but
when they have perished and are no longer here
shall I live their lives
that was so full of fear?
maybe it was anger or
even rage
because someone forgot and
let the others out of the cage
some would say it was because of pride
anyone who is not of their culture will not be allowed inside
so what's being said?
what does it all mean?
I guess desegregating these words can happen but
only in my conscious dreams
for my family
I pray that you understand
for my family I've done all that I can
I have forfeited my life
for you
my family
Where is your peace?
Where is your love?
Where is your wisdom?

Young Bloods

Chicago June 2007

how you gone heal yourself
while y'all keep gunning each other down?
5 shots fired missed their target now
another innocent victim falls to the ground!
young blood
times are hard but gone get tougher
cause you're hell bound
claustrophobic cause the hood is packed with strapped rats
now you're cell bound
hey young blood
gun shots ring out blaaaaaaw!
mistaken identity now another's been found
come on young bloods
there's got to be more love in the hood!
back in the day
we use to strap on some gloves or
fist knuckled up dripping some blood
step in our yard fucking up
you'd feel the power floods!
we too like soldiers felt we had to defend
the hood was harder back then
when we grew up (Ku Klux Klan)
except
nobody died unless they were informants
hey young blood
your potential lies deep inside you dormant
another mistaken soldier dies because of his bling
worn on him like a hood ornament!
young bloods
don't get in the ride with them fools cause blood stains are permanent
next stop the courthouse
the judge says
defendant rise in a room as silent as a mouse
sentence read by a group not of your peers
fight back them tears
as the foreman says
you ain't getting out!

they said young blood was implicated as the trigger man
though you didn't necessarily pull the trigger
the gun only has your finger prints
life as you know it will be spent
behind bars with a life sentence
young bloods
I hope these words are making sense
put down your guns and lets try to make some sense
out of all this nonsense that makes you go for broke
never to uncloak the mysteries of the free world!
the free world to roam
the world to call home!
young bloods
I'm trying to transmit some conscious love
so many messengers never make it to their destination
join in with the spirits of the Buffalo Soldiers as their souls begin this reincarnation!
fight when you absolutely have to
die cause we must
young bloods
I hope in these words
I pray you begin to trust!
what you wanna do?
young bloods

peace love wisdom

Ghost

Chicago 2009

not to be seen
except for floating around in a dream
sometimes in between the conscious state or
deep within the subconscious as you contemplate
I guess my fate was determined long ago
I feel as if I've been in this "ghost gate" before
walking around like a zombie
I took my first breath when you found me
roaming through time
searching for the love I thought I could find
crimes committed in each lifetime
accused of letting my light shine
I refuse to accept what the other people would say
declared as a witch for the last century
I've been burned at the stake
thrown into the murky depths to determine my fate
if I float then I'm lying

these waters for thousands of years are the tears I've been crying
cause every time I would drown
at the sea floor is where my truth is found
an empty shell for a snail to use my skull as his home
the only one who believed so he drug my dome along
to the edge of the seashore
again my spirit rose once more
they say ghost's tend to roam these plains because
they're not recognizing that they are no longer one of the living
some walk in shame while others are trying to live again
this ghost is just trying to find his best friend
who's name would change from lifetime to lifetime but
her eye's are the same
windows of so many yesteryears
I must have done something so wrong because
she runs in fear

when allowed within her presence
I'm treated as a peasant who cannot offer the present of love
even when I presented the hieroglyphic scroll

that was written by his Almighty from above
shoved into coffins for so many lifetimes
I feel this ghost is about to reach his prime
recognizing it's me all along I've been trying to find
no more moments of claustrophobia
this carcass shall be cremated to change the formula
I am ghost
I am the host of the spirit that shall toast life
this ghost takes breath as my wife
I ghost shall set course for new flight
Fo Flight has become my insight
the many of ghosts who channel through me
my physical self may be blind but
I ghost can see!
Ghost
I set you free!

peace love wisdom

The Ghetto

January 17th 2009 Chicago

the ghetto
the ghetto
in the ghetto, who's that young fellow?
amped up one million times past the state of mellow
with his hat half cocked
below his knees his pants are dropped
for homework
homie counts how much he made selling rocks
wants to be the king of the block
grand ma scared to go outside to the store and shop
heard that 12 year old boy got shot
right at her front door
lil homies in the hood don't seem to care no more
everybody sleeping on the floor
not cause they don't have a bed but
cause the hood got everybody scared of
the next text book drive by
bullets fly!
mama's cry
babies die
why?
the ghetto
the ghetto
I'm talking about the ghetto
who's that young fellow?
badge of honor has to be the bullet wound
the more lead received the more the product will boom!
what should read on your tomb stone
he gone
born 1999 died in 2015
survived by a mother and 2 younger brothers
somebody needs to smother these too soon to be soldiers
the ghetto's teaching them to get colder
bolder the lil homies have become
pulls out a gat and kills in the name of fun
is it because papa ain't around to discipline his little sons?
since the day shorty was born
daddy been on the run

rotting away in a prison cell like raisin in the sun
his papa's the one who actually started the pants fashion
his cell mate got lonely then started laughing
confesses his passion
to commit a sex crime

wakes up to a fiend raping him from behind
now we find lil' homies standing in line
to buy the latest gear
blinged out and for extra measure he tattoo's on his face the falling tear
about 80% of the prison population is of color so it would appear
what color you're wearing might determine
whether you live or disappear
GD's, Vice Lords, Cobra's and Latin Kings wanting to instill that fear!
In one year
500 youths were lost
growing up in the ghetto was the cost
Donny said "...know you ain't doin' what you suppose to
you doin' what you want to do
you know you hard, got to be hard!"
I say good lord!
another awaiting concrete jungle with iron bars
another generation scared
how far must we reach to catch a falling star?
standing right in front of you is where they usually are!
reach even if it's just for one
teach them that their power lies in the solar panels from the sun
waiting to fill their hearts, brains and their lungs
it matters not what ghetto you're from
let's join hands and get the job done!
in the ghetto
in the ghetto
I'm talking about the ghetto!
so rich with youth and ingenuity
help me leave behind a most beautiful legacy
about the ghetto that raised you and me!
something more positive for the children to see
It is up to we!
to free ourselves from the ghetto
I'm talking about the ghetto
the ghetto!

wisdom

Magical Puff!

Chicago 2010

puff, puff
pass, pass
come on puff, puff
pass, pass
man close that door
so I can get a contact on his drag
with stains on tip
resins burned into the lips
taking that sip
to take your mind on a trip
how you want to roll it up
blunt style or old school twist?
zig zags filled with the absolute stickiest of the ickiest!
this shit is ridiculous!
these flows keep pumping out my soul and so meticulous!
some think that 69 is just my freakiest
I might be the sneakiest motherfucker alive!
creeped up on you and stood right by your side
whispered some words that crept up inside
your dome is now my home!
wanting to take you for a ride
lets glide!
let's fly high!
cause you're sipping on the resins from my mind
they say it's a crime smoking off that dime
if this is wrong, I'm gone have to do my time

fools do exist
with a pen in hand I keep a list
in my survival mode when it's time to enlist
once again I dip
into another fatty stuffed with some that good ol' mary jane
saw that shit just before it came!
the hails would rain
I was able to brace myself and absorb the pains!
I truly began to understand
as the umbilical cord is cut
life ain't gone be the same!

babylon plucks that flower

gives it to his wife or lover hoping to gain some power

we pluck from the sticky plant

can't get caught with that cause we gone end up getting a sentence so

I keep just a smiggin"!

just enough to be twisting

we fixin' to get buzzed!

showing some Chicago Love!

Fo Flight fitting them beats to beats like a glove

my ladies in the background are the reasons the doves would cry!

they took that sip

now you feeling the dip

as they mesmerize!

tonight we all high!

high on life and how so far we've all survived!

the stains on the tips!

became the symbol of how far I'm willing to trip

the resins burned into the lips

became the mark of the fire I would spit!

taking in that sip!

traveling within this galaxy seen as me

I smoked it from the peace pipe knowing I would see!

my spirit self was revealed when I got so high

the colors in the sky bled the earth dry!

the stickiest of the ickiest told me why!

as I exhale, my mind kicks into hyper-drive!

the things on my mind

oh what they would begin to see!

don't smoke too much or I might go into the paranoia

to the umpteenth degree!

until the doors of my soul opened and

stepped out was me

approaching I was smoking!

steaming from the fire that I have spoken

as I breathed, I laced it with gasoline!

as I bit, scratched and chewed

blew a gasket and into the cosmic I flew!

stretching through time!

playing with that hocus pocus!

watching as I would disappear within the outskirts into this rhyme!

with stains on the tips and resins burned into the lips

like BJ and the Dirty Dragon

I puff! and
I puff! and
I'm just tore up!
wooooooo!
somebody take this blunt
I gotta get back to the mic!

Wisdom

Chi Town Blues

June 21 2007

welcome to the city of the Chi
you can feel the vibes as you glide
waiting to land
we do circle fly byes
the flight attendant says welcome to Chicago's O'Hare
you can take the Blue Line if
you can't afford the cab fare
straight into the heart of the Chi's downtown
keep your eye's on your shit cause
there's no lost and found
this prairie lands name at one time had a different sound
chi-ca-go, native for smelly river
dip into the waters of Lake Michigan and shiver
made it in on a cold night in Feb
wind chill was 5 below outside
felt like 10 below in the crib
this is how we sometimes live
in the city of the Chi
at one moment there's laughter
the next you hear is a sorrowful cry
we all smiled when the Bears won as Division Champs
it couldn't outweigh the other shit that would make a city damp
from blood lost because of too many lives lost to unnecessary violence
in the hood, many unsung hero's have been silenced by
good and crooked cops or
by bangers who just won't fucking stop!

if you are then
the city will pass you by
crippled and riddled by the harshness you will lie
as a homeless one on Lower Wacker Drive
trucks ride by spreading salt so drivers won't lose control
many people walk around salty cause
they say this city is so damn cold!
cold in the soul!
foot soldiers out on patrol
like grunts trying to avoid the city's crunch
watch you back cause this city packs a hell of a punch

go to the south side
don't leave your keys in the ride
your car might get you found with you still inside the trunk
you got punked!
when you took it over to the wild, wild west
I'd suggest
instead of wearing that bling dangling on your chest
you invest in a bullet proof vest
watch your back cause some fools gonna wanna put you to the test
you'll be impressed
when you come to the Pole or the North Side
get taken for an intellectualized ride
just when you thought it was cool
you get flanked and capsized!
dropped off to the East
if you can't swim
Lake Michigan has currents that will
sweep you away in her thirst feast!
you're doomed if you can't stand on your own two feet
the city is a beast with some of her lawless children on a 24/7 creep
families from housing projects displaced
segregated communities still showing levels of deep seeded self hate
tax payers constantly getting raped by
politicians who manage to escape jail time for crooked mis-takes
understand that these words are coming from a home grown
there's so much I could write in this poem but
I need to put the pen down and get back on point
stay calm in the mind and doubled in the joints!
the City of the Chi can be a tease but
I refuse to be blown away by her Windy City Breeze!
don't get me wrong
beautiful things happen here too
this just happens to be some of the
Chi Town blues!

The Great Escape

Chicago February 2011

it can never be too late
to step away from a potential tragic fate
generations have come and gone bearing the weight of
past and recycled spirits who would meditate
for centuries as they pass yet
the pain still lingers from her Magistrate
going on five hundred years!
what appears to be passive
is now in fact a spiritual gathering
that has become massive
because the medicine men read the pattern of the scattered bones
the same pieces were thrown when Babylon came and took his home!
foam develops when bitten by an animal with rabies
nothing was allowed to live
no mercy shown for the innocent babies!
salute to the red, white and the blue!
in the 21st century, the red obviously still does not refer to you!
this would be a good time for you to cast a spell of voodoo!
are the Shamans words that of patience?
just waiting?
are you still in the hills writing more cave prints to leave imprints?
not to be seen for centuries by any other on this side of existence
telling the tales of how things came to be
staying free from mental shackles
never to be bound by twisted words that leave the weak baffled
the mountains can only extend so far so
into the heavens they build a scaffold
while drinking water called Wild Turkey
how cold and murky!
within the bottle lies more than just sorrows
another meditation done to quicken the next tomorrow
is it a hibernation?
perhaps the healing of a nation!
for some déjà vu is recognition of reincarnation
do the gates of salvation or heaven exist?
how is it possible for a culture to live a mist us?
within the borders our motto says In God We Trust!
why are there no Navaho and Blackfoot openly amongst us?

the red and black cowboys left visible trails in the dust
history has also left a trail of blood that would disgust
the king of the jungle himself!
the law of the land has always been to
hunt when you must
not to go put another notch on that belt! and
the ripples continue into the next generation to be felt

how marvelous the lunar eclipse
blackberries hang from branches left for the crows to grip
red berries scattered throughout the field
oozing juice for the wolves to sip
with a list of war crimes that Babylon has pleaded the fifth?
two by two
like Noah's Ark
what a dream!
an African and Seminole as candidates as the Presidential race would start
I'm all for President Obama but
the sound of Seminole, Apache or Crete!
wisdom must be sought from the tribesman and the visions they see
they are still a surviving breed!
the great escape
why do you wait?
the blackberries have, for the most part, taken a step forward
when will you come from the hills to declare victory from the wars?
you fought so bravely when you were out numbered
please awaken from your slumber!
are you planning to take your rightful place amongst us?
I wonder!
when will you plan the great escape?
I got one more bullet in the chamber and
I gotsta pull the trigger
coming from my heart soul and liver!
let this sliver into your dome to deliver
when will my black African brothers realize they're not nigga's?
how can we justify keeping us in this mental slave trade?
we must figure out how to get out of this dilemma
while the members of the KKK are still wearing their white sheets
now it's his new soldier
knocking a culture off its feet!
with the bullet and your tongue and
that word you would keep!
when will we ever escape?

as long as you call your brother a nigga
you keep him in shackles and chained as a slave!
it's so funny cause the ones that use it the most
are always talking about another holding him down with no hope!
your brains been butt fucked after being injected with that dope!
there ain't nothing dope about hanging from a rope
while 400 plus years of generations had to cope
while being massacred
by the master!
you're building their regime faster!

while another brains splattered
back in the day
nigga's had no say
living conditions lower than dirt!
now I ask
what is your worth?
the great escape was finally planned by
the revolutionist named Harriet Tubman
hoping to return to they're rights of just being a man
as an African!
what part of the civil movement don't you understand?
Martin gave a speech that could single handedly help us advance
whether it be in sports, music, medicine or as a politician!
the world is waiting to hear the wisdom come from your mouth
what's the first thing to come out?
nigga this and nigga that!
well
the whip marks are still on your back!
with a noose that has no slack!
what's up with that?
how are we gone break away
if you keep calling your brothers a slave?
okay
you say it's a term of endearment
well that term has kept us down ever since the inception
of our government
going on 500 years
used to degrade
used to keep you as a slave
Willie Lynch said "if done properly
the masters will be able to rule you from the grave"!
free our ancestors from this eternal abomination

so deep into your mind
have you allowed the slave masters penetration
free your mind from this constant raping!
feed your soul from this starvation
this genocidal damnation!
Welcome To The Liberation!
the great escape!

Life

Chicago April 1, 2013

Life
Life
Life
Here's a little tale of life
They say what you put in is what you get out
Here I sit in meditation while dogs bark at fools who shout
About all in their lives that's going wrong
Standing still in the same hole of dong
Keys fit in the door to exit the shit so you can explore
Higher or lower
Self grower!
Chi-Town ghetto child with a spirit of ambrosia
My choice to live this lifetime a little bit slower
Sitting in temple halls with monks
who respect Buddha, Jesus, Allah, Atmu and Jehovah
cruising down the avenue in my Cordoba
listening to some sweet Bossa Nova
man, I use to be a Casanova but
Love has me tracing my path with a Super Nova
Through this galactic ponderosa
Come sit next to me on the sofa
I use to be a lyrical anorexic nervosa
Too shy to speak so a specialist came in from Nova Scotia
He gave me 69 shots of Hermosa and Vermosa
Then some "Flamin' Jamaican smoka"
Come toke a few times to ignite your mucosa
Then instructed me to journal my life so
Come a little bit closer
He said
"Write it, write it all down!
Whether it made you smile or frown
Write it all down!
Write about your life
Journal your life!
Sex me, perplex me, vex me with life
Write, write, write, write it all down Fo Flight!
Check this, check this, true story, check this
An angry child I was indeed

My Grand mama Mamie gave me my first conscious lesson on how to breathe
Remember when my "dingle ling" got caught in the zipper of my pants
You told me to take a deep breath and just as I got a chance to inhale
You snatched that zipper down and I yelled "Mama! Mama!!!"
You kissed me on the forehead and said, "it's gonna be okay!"
I swear I heard you laugh when you walked away

She said, "knuckle up, knuckle up
cause there's even more out there waiting on your butt!
Life, life
Stop crying cause no one will care about your pains
Gain knowledge from your wee-wee strain
It's life, it's life, baby, it's life
Now wipe your tears and become a man"
then she said it again
She said it's life, it's life,
baby, this is life!
Sonny was known for carrying a 44
Seven black Caddy's cruising through Lawless Gardens
looking to settle a score!
He said, "whoever they were, they won't be walking on this earth no more"
The original Black Dynamite!
Dubbed in a black maxi leather and a well groomed afro
He said, "Y'all fucked with my boys!
Who fucked with Turkey and Jimmychan. Who was it? Who was it?
We're coming deep and that's no joke'!"
With a 12 inch black barrel peeping from his coat
No dope was sold on the streets that night!
No man
He wasn't an El Rukin, Panther or Black Stone Ranger but
Man, he could float like a ghost
He always would tote
that midnight blue pearled handled magnum ready to smoke!
From 1969 to '94, the book on "Street Hustle" you better believe he wrote
He said
"don't act like no bitch!
Let's go watch some Bruce Lee so you can learn how to kick life's ass!
4:30 am wake up call to see a full moon and sunrise then bask
let no man put fear in your heart or treat you like trash
if you don't know, motherfucker you better ask!"
He said, "It's just life, it's life, it's all about life
It's 'dia-flakey of the blow hole'
It's all about life

It's life, it's life
Now hand me my knife
I'm gonna help you to whittle your life
It's All about life!
Spirit Life"

Peace Love and Wisdom

Night, Night

September Chicago 2007

Night, night
I hope you enjoyed the flight
though left and forgotten while on the runway
I will silently rock the mic
through the airwaves I'm putting up a fight
a battle that resides deep within
should I pack up my bags and call it a day
knowing you were never truly a friend
how could I pretend to act as if I wasn't phased
had 2 drinks of that blue pill so
just like yours, I'm sure is was written all over my face
probably traces of tequila and laces of some mary jane
on the runway I sit hoping to rain on the mic just for you
as a friend I felt obligated to do the do!
sensuous September!
I was ready to deliver a theme for all to remember
guaranteed to make the audience cream!
added with some holla's and screams, sighs, moans and
you know me!
Ready to put that extra twist then
seal it with the Fo Flight kiss
sit back cause you on the list so no need to panic
god damn it, 69 ink spots all over my body should hint that
I might be one of the freakiest brothers
within five solar systems and their existing planets
maybe thought to be a manic depressant

too many think that I'm just a rebel professing
I've been type cast so this flight has once again been put on hold or
better phrased, I'm a fighter jet instead of a an airbus so
there will be a slight delay
the nights almost up and several poets have had a chance to say
at least 2 even 3 pieces
about a whole lot of fucking and sucking and some conscious loving
why does Chicago not love her own and keep shoving
her seeds into the cradle of another
like Kanye had to fly the coup to be discovered
found out he too likes to take away another's moment of thunder

common sense would tell you a brother ain't a brother
because his color of royal blue with dragons prints
an unmistakable nag champa scent

an aura that radiates with content
sometimes you make me feel like I'm getting pimped
you know, like a poet hoe
the one who
gets paid no dough but geeked up to perform at every show
there is no way you can forget one of your loyal soldiers
one who would stop time just to rub your head, back and shoulders
with my physical chi flow or lyrics from my eclectic mental folder
falls coming and the seasons feeling colder
bolder I must become
like only a true Chicago son
run forest run!
with all this concrete around me stifling my veins
like Rafeal Saddiq "I'm leaving this town" cause
I can't find no true love in this Chicago poetry scene
strange how they call out your name
playing that popularity game
some things just never change
one things for sure
here I can no longer remain
now that's a shame!
that's why I like to pay my way
tonight I think I've been shown an alternate destiny
I wish you absolute success in your present and future journey
please don't think that my feelings were hurt
it's just another reminder that I wont be last on the list nor the first
there's nothing in the middle so possibly cursed to never make the list again
why can't this native of the Chi be one of her pimped out friends
instead I've been chosen to be her knight and sent out to slay the dragon
some say "dude you need to calm down"
others have suggested that only in my mind am I Hollywood bound
while many, many others have found through the pages of my manuscripts
I absolutely flip the script with some of the freakiest shit that
you will ever come to hear in this lifetime!
romantic, lustfully sinful
pages that could make a sour stale dark pussy turn to sunshine!
another moment not to claim as mine so back on the grind
mind, body and soul
Peace Love Wisdom

Black Butterflies

Chicago August 2012

Black butterflies
Use to spread them wings and glide
In the Asiatic sunrise
Became the prize of mystery Babylon
Who enslaved, preyed then gave him another name
NIGGER!
Now the order has been engraved
A sentence of brutality and genocide
Babies can't go outside and just play cause
The fury of mystery Babylon is coming their way
Babies cry cause mama and daddy are about to die
Cause they dared to dream like Harriet Tubman and
Free slaves in the Underground railroad in the pitch black night
Cracking hips and whips
while bodies are hung by a noose and burned to a crisp
black butterflies wings have been clipped
tagged as the lowest of the low so
they were dropped off in the Atlantic sea to sink to the floor with whale shit
equipped with some Willy Lynch
now it all makes sense
Adidas designed some gym shoes with shackles on them to drop another hint
Prison systems overpopulated with 35 percent of an entire generation
Another holocaust to curve the population
Executed with precision and patience
Black butterflies have been devoured
A new Jim Crow has planted a seed of self hate so deep

Mystery Babylon's been observing in his watch tower
Been putting them glocks and rocks in little homies pockets
Filled with cash money that pimps out young black men
Baring their asses!
Rewarded with lashes
From a system that practices this technique called supremacy
Claiming God gave them clemency
Wake up black butterflies
Why can't you see?

Black butterflies spread your wings and be free
Awaken black butterflies, you gotta try to break free
From this hybrid cocoon
Souls marooned on this island ship
Being groomed
Instead of caterpillars
30 to 40 percent of black men been placed in them cells and are dubbed as maggots
Another Tuskegee Experiment to breed black men
into gays, closet queers and fagots
That's what THEY call you man, that's what they call you!
Every variation of an altered self
The next ripple felt is the woman contracting A.I.D.S and
the system knows who's got it
Like the roach motel, a device designed to kill the main cell
Send the poison back into the Queens layer to kill all in sight
Black Butterflies
Spread your wings
Fly
Fly get up and try!
Black Butterflies
Get up off your knees
Stop your crying while in your sleep
It's time to face your true destiny!

Peace Love Wisdom

Sweet Jesus

Chicago, May 2013

Blinded in the dark
Which way do I start?
Left or right can be a dead end or spark
More time spent deep in a cave
For pulses of love deep in the heart
Lions, tigers and bears scare the average man into the recesses of fear
Tears well up in an instant coffee brewed
To the tune of footsteps by this well kept secret of a man
ChanClan etched in deep colors of the spectrum
That radiates prisms of magnificent energy that blesses them
Who wants to be bathed by spirits such as John of God?
Snobs and disbelievers
Call us the deceivers
Who would lead a child into war to make the mother a griever?
Leave a letter of Purple Hearts and moments of valor
Scour terrain where man dance the dance causing blood to rain
Under cloudless sky's
Babies cries, fathers, sons, mothers and daughters die twice
First the soul becomes blackened from taking another's life
Then the mind is trapped in a moment while paying the price
As it repeats to creep into ones sleep
Sweet Jesus
Rock me to sleep
Sweet Buddha come and meditate with
Allah, Jah Rastafari
Anybody from the higher side
Post traumatic syndrome is diagnosed to the killer beast
Always aim for the sweet spot in this war game of kill or be killed
Government trained to be skilled in pulling triggers
Hollow tips in the hands of more tribal, sand and ghetto igga's
Penitentiaries housing an overwhelming figure of
Blindly innocent souls while the real perpetrators
Sit in Senate seats and continue to disfigure
A woman's body belongs to her

Laws written on murdered trees and now processed pieces of papers
Takers of mind body and soul
For social security

Is your number for the undertaker
Remembering the lives lost in the Holocaust
Numbers etched into the flesh and spirits tossed
Into flames while family and friends whisper their name
Africans bred in the Americas ashamed of heritage
Brainwashed to treat his bredren like wild game
Stuck in freeze frame and
Again the bullets rain
Songs on the radio use to sing of love supreme
Coltrane is high as kite!
Ku Klux Klan gave him a reason to play every note about this luscious life
Bright tomorrow still comes
Mental shackles still worn by some
Light and darkness becomes a perception
Feed not on your fellow man but the brilliant rays from the sun
Remember each day you're allowed to see
Know this life is almost done
I just have one simple request before that day
Please Put Down Your Guns!
Please Put Down Your Guns!
Please!
No more bombs
This one goes out to Boston!
Sweet Jesus rock me to sleep!
Sweet Jesus rock me to sleep
Sweet Buddha come meditate with me
Whisper into the a child's ear something sweet!
Lift them from off their knees and onto their feet!
Sweet Jesus, Allah, Buddha, Jah Rastafari!
I don't care whomever you are!
Sweet Jesus rock me to sleep
Sweet Jesus, Sweet Buddha
Allah, Jehovah
Even if you're an Atheist
You must do something that can help us!

Peace Love Wisdom

Look Within

Chicago January 2, 2014

Like mama earth
The body's composition is a majority of water
God assigned her to be mans porter
Within the vastness we stand here as sons and daughters
On every border man gives nickles, dimes and quarters to mystery babylon
So he can continue to slaughter
We ought to know that fossil fuel is the blood given by the father
Man robs her blind
Look into the bottom of the ocean and guess what you gonna find
You're gonna find reflections of greed, hate and lust
Dust in the water and wind because of the fathers disgust
You're gonna find
Barrels of radioactive waste
Fish taste mans haste
Now the pace is hyper-accelerated
With so many species being erased
Like an episode of "Lost in Space"
Debris from centuries
Mans destiny
With so much hate in his heart instead of preserving life
Murder becomes his ecstasy
Ancestral spirits stand next to me
Asking for a cup of sweet tea
Trees cut down to build mansions for rich single family's
While other species live in this diaspora
From the Amazon rainforest to Angola
The Americas to China
What will it take to change this formula?
You must look within
And guess what you're gonna find
You're gonna find reflections of greed, hate and lust
Dust in the water and wind because of the fathers disgust
They say guns don't kill but
Put it into the hands of an ill willed man then blood is gonna spill
Like the drills driving, deep sea diving
thru the belly of mama earths underwater gills
like video games teaching children murderous skills
Man is still burning crosses on them hills

Wake up my brothers and sisters
You took the blue instead of the red pill!
I'm gonna keep reciting from the ink spilled
Hoping these words of insight can fill your hearts with good will
Look within
Look within…
Peace Love and Wisdom

The World Around You

Chicago, January 10, 2014

Look at the world around you
Filled with pimps, hustlers and fools
To the youth and young MC's, it's time for this Black Dynamite
To take you to the old school
Pools of knowledge cause I attended a 4 year college
Dropped out in 2 ½ cause it was time to acknowledge
Time to pay respect and homage to the World University
Here comes some Fo Flight69 Rhapsody
So honest while trekking around to see so many people with so much in common
Everybody wants the cheese so they can live in the penthouse or deluxe cottage
Step into 3rd world lands where they've got it the hardest
No food with the poorest in shelter but
with a smile on their faces while 15 are living in a crib the size of a closet
Living conditions so bad it might make you vomit
Did you know that the cost of your Nikes
could feed an entire family's empty stomach?
hummus would be nice but in Mama Africa
They are treated as if they're the dumbest
Tuskegee experiments now testing deep in the Congo
Hear the rhythm of the bongos
While A.I.D.S is dropping them like dominoes
Not many children get to grow and know that mama was gang raped
By a bunch of 12 year olds who were forced to put on this show
Don't you know you are birthed from Gods DNA?
Your gene pool comes from cosmic dust birthed way out in outer space
Bone marrow from Pharaohs and descendants of Queens and Kings

Mystery Babylon put all this material shit in front of you to block the doors
Blocking you from discovering your Lord
You, Yourself and The First Eye
Try harder youngins' cause you gotta put up a better fight
You gotta look at the world around
Don't let it beat you down to the ground
Know that you can be whatever you wanna be
Come and help me!
Help me teach
Help to set some soul captives free!

Think in a process to make things better Overstood
You gotta really think about how all them guns got into your hood
Would it be a coincidence the rest of the world is also living in suspense?
Military defense weapons issued by the most powerful government
Making sure there will be no more descendants
Imprisonment imposed for selling dime bags of weed
Power hungry banks bleed out the people then receive
A bailout so they can afford the next trick up their sleeves
Bombs exploding in them Boston streets
Take a look around you now come marathon run with me
Cause you gotta awaken from your deep sleep
Babylon don't won't peace
He's supplying every hustler on every world block and corner
With guns, drugs and poverty
This is the lesson he's trying to teach

Peace Love and Wisdom

The Other Side of Midnight

Chicago and New York April 15-21 2013

Hear the daughters and son cry cause
Mamas about to go into flight
Body beat down because something inside ain't right
She puts up an ultimate fight!
She's a liver and a giver but
The liver has become a taker
God don't make her go away
Cancer is in retrograde and there she lay
Feeling the energy from Michelle, LuLu Le'moon and me
One more loving touch then she'll be free
Now she's on the other side of midnight
And she's ready to fly!
She's on the other side of midnight
You can hear the rain pouring outside
She's on the other side of midnight
You can hear the angels cry
She's on the other side
On the other side
Blessings Rosalba
It was an absolute honor to be allowed to stand before you sharing energy
Your presence of spirit, I felt burning strong in my right knee
Blessings upon the we allowed to absorb some of your power yin chi
Preparing for the flight into this heavenly molecular sea
We must have met some life time ago
Maybe the roles were reversed and you blessed my soul
Blessings to you Rosalba

She's on the other side of midnight
And she's ready to fly!
She's on the other side of midnight
You can hear the rain pouring outside
She's on the other side of midnight
You can hear the angels cry
She's on the other side
On the other side

Now she's taking an inward journey to help learn we
The vessel of she

Every mans destiny evolves around Her-story
History only tell lies disguised in brutality
While mama earth houses the sea's
Oceans, mountains and trees
Where seed are fertilized
Sky's filled with oxygen
Only inhale goodness in your life and leave out the toxins
Know beside all strong men stood a strong woman boxing
All his demons so
His seeds shall breed again the next generations of spirits!

She's on the other side of midnight
And she's ready to fly!
She's on the other side of midnight
You can hear the rain pouring outside
She's on the other side of midnight
You can hear the angels cry
She's on the other side
On the other side
Peace Love Wisdom Flight

Welcome to Chiraq

Chicago March 2012

Welcome to Chiraq

Chi-town

My town

Come and drown in these lyrical minds that produces such a funky sound

While you're riding these waves

Hold on tight or you might be found

Up a creek

Chicago's known for some of her positive peeps

Special dedication to Mr. Bernie Mac

My brother, Rest In Peace -_-

Oh yes, let me show some respect

To our Mr. President

To the rest of the world, here's a present from Chicago that we've sent

Mr. President Barack Hussein Obama!

Gone Mr. President, gone represent!

Back in the day this would have been something that sounded kinda freaky

Within the good we also got some "sneaky deaky's"

They push up on you while you're feeling sleepy

She's walking and not paying attention on that cell phone and just keeps talking

For six blocks a man in blacks been stalking

Now the laws chalking

Another body found in the hawking wind of the Chi

You gotta stay on point if you wanna stay alive

I know this shit happens everywhere but I'm talking about the Chi!!!

They could pick up a spliff and just lounge

Instead, homie picks up a gat and now he's cell bound!

Chi-Town pimped out with some of them windy city frowns

You push up on the wrong one and you going down and down

Pushing up them daisies and crack vials six feet underground

Chicago! My town!

Dear Mr. President

I have mad love for who you are in spirit and the Legacy you represent.

I wish mom and gramps could have been alive in this era to watch you ascend with purpose into the Big White House. I overstand your work bares of difficult tasks. I just simply ask, please don't forget about us! Your Hometown! Our Children are being slaughtered at an alarming rate and we need your support and help!

Sincerely,

ChanClan

Peace Love and Wisdom

No More War

Chicago July, 2013

Whether you're a Muslim or a Christian
You can vibe upon this one
Whether you're a black or a white man
You can vibe upon this one
This verse goes out to the politicians
I really think you don't give a damn!
Blood flows throughout the land
You won't stretch out a healing hand
You want us to follow your plan
Sweet Lord, even God you damn
Remember what you did to Japan?
Now you're dropping them bombs in Afghanistan
They know what you did to the Africans
Call them the terrorists while you spill blood in their sand
Why must we endure this selfish war?
No more war!
No more war!!!
Whether you're a Muslim or a Christian
You can vibe upon this one
Whether you're a black or a white man
You can vibe upon this one
Bang! Bang! Bang!
They shot another one down!
Killed him in the name of fun
Glory to the gangs full of fatherless sons

Pants sagging past his knees so its impossible to run
Yet another ploy by mystery Babylon
Bullets rain from military issued guns
Why won't you allow the police to bring in them 20 ton tanks
You shun your own so he can't cast his vote
Cause he's traded it in for ammunition
Now the war is in them ghetto's
Mother's against daughters
Lifetime sentences reconnect fathers and sons
No more war!

No more war!!!
Whether you're a Muslim or a Christian
You can vibe upon this one
Whether you're a black or a white man
You can vibe upon this one
No more war Bob Marley would sing!
Till this day the wicked still constantly brings

Bloodshed and poverty as the gunshots ring
Like the winter and summer seasons bring change
For over 400 years the black man is still feeling the strain
No rice or grain
Blacks rise up and liberate yourselves from these mental chains
No more Lil Wayne's to be a role model for our children because
they're becoming Baby Jane's
turning into same sex offenders to pass on to the next generation
who will possibly do the same
No more war!
No more war!!!
Bob Marley Said No More War!!!
Whether you're a Muslim or a Christian
You can vibe upon this one
Whether you're a black or a white man
You can vibe upon this one
War in the East
War in the West
War up North
War down South
Conscious people of mother earth, it's time to open up your mouths!
It's time to kick the wicked out
Ring the bell of consciousness
It's time to Shout!
There's a love drought
Too much self doubt
What is your chosen route?
No more war, no more war!
Love and Peace is what we're searching for!
War in the East
War in the West
War up North
War down South No more war!
No more war!!!

Bob Marley Said No More War!!!
Whether you're a Muslim or a Christian
You can vibe upon this one
Whether you're a black or a white man
You can vibe upon this one

Peace Love and Wisdom

Cool Summer Breeze

Chicago July 2013

As I ease my way into a conscious stream of
Wind creating ripples and currents
Rivers, lakes, oceans and sea's
Polluted like the minds filled with feces
I sneeze cause of negative debris
Coming out of the mouths of human species
Allergic to caca so a vegetarian diet becomes so easy to swallow
Hollow trees sway in the wind into the next tomorrow
I follow cycles of the moon while others feed on sorrows
Borrow truths from the philosophers who spits in the booth
Deuce is good for more than 3
We spit to set free any ear
That wants to soar into the galaxy's to step away from mama earths streets
Where bullets fly to drop Kings and Queens and deplete her cosmic tranquility
Cool Summer Breeze
Help set me free
Cool summer breeze
I wanna be yea
Cool summer breeze
Help set me free yea
Cool summer breeze
I wanna be yea!
Allow me to become we
Fo Flight
Bringing love, peace and harmony
Sincerity to the 69th degree
Alas we are truly free
I am that summers breeze that ruffles through the leaves
Dancing on your flesh and tickling you at any angle that I please
Tickling your eardrums just from the sound of me
See!
My invisible form comes to life as the mighty tree
Sways!
And every living organism gets to inhale
My essence and be bathed with cosmic dust from every galaxy known and unknown

Cool Summer Breeze
Help set me free

Cool summer breeze
I wanna be, yea
Cool summer breeze
Help set me free, yea
Cool summer breeze

I am the same wind that blew
When pharaohs set the slaves free
As the sea's would part to create the Serengeti
360 degrees swirl to create mountains from loose debris
Heated by solar blasts emitting
From the sun's solar electricity of
Heat waves warming currents to the seashore
I am the reason you love the great outdoors
Even when the artic blast takes over and freezes your pipes and floors
As sure as the sky is blue
I Santa Anna Winds blow in a rhythmic breath just for you
Come breathe of me
Soak me into your physical and feel your spirit so when it's time for you to fly
Flow with me 3rd Eye

Cool Summer Breeze
Help set me free
Cool summer breeze
I wanna be, yea
Cool summer breeze
Help set me free, yea
Cool summer breeze

Peace Love Wisdom

Blaze Jah Fire

New York February 2013

Strike a flame from my favorite bic lighter
Put it to my face just before I began to spit
Lyrics would glow and illuminate higher
Where dragons breath meets the sun to create this ultimate fire
Of Spit!
This natural gasoline is firing off from the tip of my spirit
To depths of my bubbling spring, tickling my toes
Flows of poetry
On the count of 3
This Shaolin technique is called "Torch The Galaxy"
Blaze Jah fire so his mama can see!
Welcome to the Dragons Den!
Blaze it
I'm gonna blaze Jah fire now!
Blaze it, blaze it!
Fo Flights about to blaze a fire now!
Born into this city known for its wind
Where everybody's trying to be a king pen
Drips on paper to waste another tree
Lit just before I spit like a governments experiment that went so wrong
I write them blaze a fire kind of songs
Chi-Towns home grown!
Flown around the world to be shown
Like Malcolm in the Mecca
Invest a moment of meditation
Now be patient cause it's time to get your swag on!
Tag on I can tongue press the blazing sun
Dragon Balls are spit for the pure pleasure and fun
Shaolin Temples Prodigal Son
Blazing Jah fire since time
You be gun
I'll be liquid sword
Created by the lord began dams of ink
From my freaky cool think tank of spirit gold bullion brink links
To the spirit dwellers
Who bathe in spit of dragons who tell a sweet blaze of fire
From the scales of the spine to the heights and depths of the heavens and hell
Blaze a Fire!

Blaze it! Fo Flight's about to blaze a fire now!
East, West, North and South
This blaze is ready to come from the dragons mouth
It burns, it burns, it burns!!!

Be Like Water

Chicago February 17, 2014

Look into the heavenly glory
Empty your mind
Be like water
Be like water my friend
Be water
Here I stand at the alter
Incense burning to invite spirits so I can talk to
Meditations to clear my mind so it won't bother
Me, myself and third eye
Shower me heavenly father
Quench my thirst so that I might blossom like a flower
Point me to the river bed to meet the spirit talkers
I don't wanna drink no more Johnny Walker
I need to be bathed by a tsunami stalker
Covering about 71 percent of mama earth
Just like her sons and daughters
Swig on 8-10 glasses a day just like you ought to
It don't matter if you're filthy rich or a pauper
Man, you need to be like water
Be water, be water
Look to the heavenly glory and empty your mind
Be like water
Be water my friend
Since the beginning
You've been swimming
Like a nut traveling up stream
While that egg was just chilling
6 elements of you designed from some freaking
oxygen, carbon, calcium, phosphorus and hydrogen
9 months later mamas water came spilling
This is an innate biological trait
this ain't up for debate
who dares argue with drops of water as it runs down your face
subtle as a train wreck
when a billion drops times infinity forms to create
oceans, rivers, ponds, lakes and seas
you gotta blow and flow with the currents rippling in the breeze

Look to the heavenly glory
Now empty your mind
Be like water
Be water
Be water my friend
Be water and take on the shape of a teapot
Become formless to stream through and around mountaintops
Crash into the seashores and never stop
Become the shape of a tub while boiling hot
As it drip drops
Becoming the key hole as the pressure unlocks
I water will spit this harder than 2 Pac
Flow smooth like Bob Marley and Peter Tosh
Be the twin dragon spirit of Bruce Lee's nunchucks
Be like water my friend so
nothing can disrupt
Nothing can corrupt this fluid
Allow the currents to flow to rid you of all your sewage
Close your eyes and become intuitive
Be the rolling tidal waves so lucid
Keep you opponent clueless and stupid
All shapes and forms are excluded
Let them be the rock
Stoned on tainted pot
while your spirit stays nice and wet
With confidence and absolutely no regrets
Don't forget my friend

Be like water
Be water
Be water my friend
Be water
Behold the heavenly glory and empty your mind
Be water...

The captain has turned off the fasten seat belt signs
Next stop
How about multiple drop off spots?
From the beaches of Jamaica
To give thanks and praises with Rastafari and
Them conscious dredlocks
How about some fine dining in Thailand's Bangkok?
Learn some ultimate kickboxing with Ong Bak

Maybe go and climb the tallest African or Australian Rock
Breathe into a didgeridoo while under water in mountain springs bubbling hot
Man, I gotta go to China's Shaolin
Take me deeper into some spirit training
3rd Eye Wu Tang 69
Fo Flight eagle flying, soaring through the heavens while Frankie's Blazin'
Another moment praising this microphone
Every note takes me home
Deep into my dome
Yes, lets go meditate and
Be Like Water…
Peace Love and WISDOM

Time Spent Alone 69

Time
Just a little bit of time
I do truly apologize for the delay
You'd never believe what happened to me and my lady
Alternate route on I-90 so we could come back to Chicago and play
Now we're trying to forget that shit way back at the toll gate
Bordered by a Canadian mist that set a path while cruising on the highway
Pit stop to Niagara Falls
Drops of water can hide tears on my face in such a place
Space bend a moment in time
Déjà vu or totally erase I
This crooked and corrupted government
7 G's spent at a border
call it harassment
now I'm a dissident running from the law on a cross continent chase
Jesus nailed on a cross looking at me like he spent time alone

Time spent alone, time spent, time spent alone
You need to meditate
Time spent alone
You need to meditate to find yourself
Time spent alone
Get away from all this bullshit
Time spent alone
Go deep, go deep and find yourself
Time spent alone
Go deep, go deep and find yourself
You need some time alone
It's all a lie
No need to ask the questions why

Time
Time to go back home
Maybe journey to the land where the didgeridoo is blown
Should I even journey to the temple where the Shaolin Monks call home
Maybe swim to Tahiti or Fiji
Meditate with the forests in Bali
I be all alone searching for me

No more security codes
Fold my legs into lotus and behold
Time spent alone to realize my heavenly soul
Run Forest run from all trying to seize control
Blow in the eight directional winds and boldly go where man is afraid to grow
It is only I that me and myself should know

Time spent alone
It's just time, it's just time
Time spent alone
Find your own way
Time spent alone
Time spent alone
Time spent alone
Maybe to sit in Damo's cave!
Learn how to breathe
Deep within
Time spent alone
In an Arhat posture alone
Time spent alone
Gazing at the stars
Time spent alone
It's essential to understand how the wicked man behaves
Living deep within his rage
See's the eagle soaring through the sky
Now he wants to capture him and put him is his cage
In a prison cell filled with lost souls who've lost their way to Damo's cave
Engrave your likeness as an inmate to make you lifeless
Fight this!
Within the darkness every star in the galaxy is seen
Ultra brightness!
Mental Skype this
Stretch your limbs with the Lohan to release your mental and physical tightness
Third eye write this Sutra to the Dragon
For it bares a likeness of my true self
cause I spend my time alone
Alone
Time spent alone
My time spent alone
I need this time alone to do some yoga
Do my favorite Asana
Time spent alone
Do some Tai Chi and get to know me and the tree's, the birds and the bee

Alone
Spend it alone, Spend it alone
Time, time, time, time, time, time, time, time, time, time, time, time, time, time, time
Time spent alone
Spend it alone
Take your time, find your mind
Feel the sun and moonshine
Spend the time Alone
Peace, Love and Wisdom

69

I hope you've enjoyed the tour of my mind. If you hadn't noticed, the Red Pill was swallowed for these writings. Each time I took the Red Pill, it was accompanied with this sweet sensation from the "Cup of Love"

Cup of Love

Chicago January 1st 2011

If I don't try
I'll just die
Never knowing who lived inside
Between these eyes lies a soul that's danced here before
Traveling through those 8th Dimensional Doors
Explored the Lord known as I
He, She maybe even an Hermaphrodite
Gave me some insight to the Yin and Yang
She said all the problems going on the surface of Mother Earth is mans been sprung
Fucked Mama so good based on his greed
Now Mama's going to bleed to death
Each time she heals herself another blow is felt from man
Cause
Man can heal
He can steal
He can kill
Bring babies into the world or
Burn crosses on them hills but
Can he refill this cup of love
Can you stop spilling yours and Mama Earths blood
Five Hundred kids where killed in the course of one year
on these Chi-Town city blocks
caught between this big ass rock spinning
while the others rocks are stealing
from communities for mystery Babylon who refuses to stop
I can't say for sure your Honor cause

after glock, after glock, after glock, after block, after block, after block
the sound of gunshots where another innocent bystander gets popped
blood flows into far away lands where they get them heads chopped off
why can't we just talk?
Thoughts of massacre can't be the way you actually want to deal
Look into the eyes of a child then you'll know exactly the reason why not to spill!

I say
Man can heal
He can steal
He can kill

Bring babies into the world or
Burn crosses on them hills but
Can he refill this cup of love
Can you stop spilling yours and Mama Earths blood!

The blood of man still flows through the land
Mama said she can't stand y'all no more so she don't give a damn!
She's gonna grandstand the Homo Sapiens
With floods and earthquakes
Volcanic eruptions and eyes of Hurricanes
That look like spinning wheels
That kills all in its path
To Libya, Pakistan, Iraq, Iran, Africans, China man!
Europeans and Americans! Israel! Israel! Palestinians!
Put down your weapons of mass destruction cause
Everybody Just Needs A Good Strong Dose of Loving!!!

I say
Man can heal
He can steal
He can kill
Bring babies into the world or
Burn crosses on them hills but
Can he refill this cup of love
Can you stop spilling yours and Mama Earths blood!
One more time, ONE MORE TIME!
Man can heal
He can steal
He can kill
Bring babies into the world or
Burn crosses on them hills but
Can he refill this cup of love
Can you stop spilling yours and Mama Earths blood!
Say it one more time!
Man can...

Peace Wisdom Cup of Love -_-

Coming Up Next:

6 "Kama Sutra" 9

Printed in the United States
By Bookmasters